Long Gone

LONG GONE

RICHARD WILLIS

Greenpoint Press

Sections of this book have appeared in Ducts Webzine.
www.ducts.org

Cover and book design by Rob Kimmel Design
www.robkimmeldesign.com

The text of this book is set in Scala, designed by Martin Majoor.
Cover title is hand-set wood type proofed at The Center for Book Arts, New York City

Cover photo: the author (l.) and Morey (on tractor)

ISBN 0-9759760-2-8

Greenpoint Press
A subsidiary of New York Writers Resources
PO Box 3203
Grand Central Terminal
New York, NY 10163

www.newyorkwritersworkshop.com
www.ducts.org

Printed in the United States of America

Long Gone is dedicated to my wife, Linda Barry Willis, for her patience and support through the months and years this project has been underway, for her keen editorial comments and positive suggestions, and to Charles Salzberg, the best teacher I have ever known, for his encouragement and ingenuity in bringing the memoir to its final form.

Acknowledgments

First on the list of those who have contributed their time and energy to *Long Gone*, must be Jonathan Kravetz. I am also indebted to members of Charles Salzberg's writing classes, who read the manuscript and made suggestions for its improvement: Vivian Conan, Betty Wald, Victoria Reggio, Sally Koslow, Lauren Weisberger, and Ricki Miller.

I'd also like to thank Bonnie Jacobs Lindenmayer, my unfailing source of information about people and places in Marengo.

And to those whose generosity made this book possible: Fred Abraham, Molly Algermissen, Dom Angiello, Jennifer M. Armstrong, Loryn Ashley, Vivienne Avramoff, Lara Bazelon, Peter Bernhardt, Valerie M. Block, Joan Bowman, Barrie Brett, Ellen Brooks, Katharine Butler, Sandra P. Chamson, Vivian Conan, Patty Dann, Barbara DeShong, Richard Dubin, Susan Durham, Susan J. Edsall, Susan Falk, Benjamin Feldman, Diane Flynn, The Ford Foundation, Laura Fuerstein, Christopher Galati, Doug Garr, Mark Gasper, Mark Goldblatt, Marilyn Goldstein, Judith A. Gorfain, Susan Gurman, Sharon Gurwitz, Stephanie R. Hart, Aileen Hewitt, Sally Hoskins, Sandra Hurtes, Inna Idelchik, Daniel Katz, Margaret H. Kennedy, Mary Kirby, Judy Knudtson, Leslie Koeppel, Beth Kwon, Christina Meldrum, Tom Morneau, Brian Mori, Julie Negrin, Leslie Nipkow, Helen Rafferty, Sharron Reakhof, Marian Sabat, Ellen Schecter, Sherry Shaw, Erika V. Shearin Karres,Wayland Stallard, Tim Tomlinson, Mary Elizabeth Wald, Virginia B. Wallace, Lori and Bill Willis, Helen Zelon.

I'd also like to thank Rob Kimmel for his creativity, inspiration and hard work in designing this book.

Introduction

Long Gone is what I can recall of growing up on an Iowa farm between 1933 and 1947. Readers looking for our lost rural culture, the source of those family values you hear so much about, will find some of it here.

Farmers like to talk about their independence, never mind that they are shackled to their livestock and to the land they work. Bonds that strong have dragged me back to the place I so badly wanted to leave when I was young. The old folks warned me I would change my mind about life on the farm. I never believed them.

So few farmers are left today the Census no longer has a category for them. Family-size farms are at best hazy memories, the subjects of politicians' lies. *Long Gone* provides a glimpse of what life was like on an old-time farm and in a small town nearby.

The Odd Fellows Cemetery
Near Marengo, Iowa
February 23, 1991

We were burying my younger bother, Morey Willis, and when we turned into the cemetery, a line of cars, their headlights on as part of the funeral procession, stretched back as far as I could see. His many friends had come to pay their respects. Morey's oldest son, Bill, said he'd never seen that many of his father's gang dressed up, and looking so uncomfortable. Somebody at the funeral home said the same thing about Morey.

Frederick Morrison Willis was born on a cold, gray day in November 1938. His elaborate name came from my wanting him to be named for our grandfather, and from some unexplained connection our mother had to a family named Morrison. Morey and I were born eleven years apart.

Our parents were tenant farmers working 185 acres of third-rate land, struggling in the grip of what seemed to be a never-ending Depression. There was neither electricity nor running water in our farmhouse. The coming war had not yet made itself felt in rising farm prices.

When Morey was born, our parents were too old (Maude was forty-two; Aubrey a year younger) and too ground down by work to cope with a rambunctious little boy. While Maude made no secret of not wanting a second child, Aubrey seemed sheepishly proud of having fathered another son at the age of forty-one, and responded to teasing with, "I was really only fooling." As for me, I'd been the only kid in the family for more than eleven years. I thought I had first claim to whatever might make life easier or more amusing, and I didn't want to share any part of it with a newcomer.

"What about this new brother of yours? What do you think about that?"

"I'd a lot rather have a pony," I said.

"Oh, now, you don't want to talk like that."

Ah, but I did. I really did.

Although I was nearly twelve years old, I hadn't been told about my mother's pregnancy. Maude took care to prepare me for our move to the farm, and later for some minor surgery I had to undergo, but she kept her condition a secret. I wasn't the only one she hid it from; some of our neighbors didn't know that she was pregnant. Even to begin to understand this nonsense, you have to remember that it was before the start of World War II and women like my mother were thought to be past the age for childbearing. Maybe she was embarrassed about her condition.

From the time we first moved to the farm, my mother made me an ally in her battles with Aubrey. I was afraid of my father, hated the work he made me do and, probably for that reason, could never please him. I took my mother's side in their never-ending battles, bawling my head off along with her. Relations with my father never improved.

Neither Maude nor Aubrey could bring themselves to tell me about the impending birth, and I probably would not have accepted it if they had. (Sigmund, where were you when we needed you?) My mother told me she was going to the hospital for a rest, and I believed her, and that was the last time I believed anything either of my parents told me.

I was sent to town to stay with my grandparents, always a big treat, and I was alone in the house with my grandma early the next morning when Aubrey drove up. He said something to Mom that I couldn't hear. Mom was deaf, and I guess she couldn't hear him either, because he tore a check in half, and wrote on the back of it, "Boy. Eight pounds. You tell Dick." Then, in character, he fled, leaving my grandma to deal with a kid who felt betrayed, and was howling to heaven about it.

In the long run, my brother and I got along better together than anybody else in the family, probably because we grew up treating each other like strangers, which is exactly what we were.

A funeral is a good place to see ghosts, so when someone touched me on the arm, and I found Maury Hartz standing there, I jumped. I thought he was dead. When I was a kid, Maury seemed like an adult to me, taller and more mature than the rest of us. Now he looked short and stocky.

"My God, Maury, how long has it been since the last time I saw you?"

"Dick...." He didn't seem to know what to say next. "I was sorry to hear about Morey."

His voice was unnaturally high and thin. Maury loved machinery, especially tractors, but tractors weren't equipped with mufflers until years after we were first on the farm. The day-in-day-out blast of sound had wrecked his hearing.

"Well, thank you." I tried to shift the subject a little, and make it easier for him to talk. "You know, you are the very first person I met from this neighborhood. Remember that muddy night, I guess it must have been the winter of 1931 or '32, when we got stuck with the my granddad's Model-T, and you came along and gave us a hand?"

"Sure I do remember that. It was before the old house burned," said Maury.

"That's right, it was. You know, I never did see that house, but I heard a lot about it from Maude."

"Gosh, that was a long time ago."

He really said Gosh. One of the remarkable things about Maury was that, alone among the men in our neighborhood, he didn't swear.

We exchanged a little more uneasy conversation, and he drifted off into the crowd at the graveside, leaving me alone with my memories of Morey, my mother, my father, and the farm.

Where the Trouble Started
Iowa 1921

Maude Karsten and Aubrey Willis, the people soon to be my parents, were married in a civil ceremony in April 1921. They started their lives together farming on land they rented from Aubrey's father, George Willis.

During the mid-1920's, terrible floods in the Mississippi River basin washed out their crops several years in a row. Looking for a less risky way to make a living, Aubrey took a job with Maude's uncle in Dallas, Texas, a clerical position with Famous Players, a film distribution company formed by a group including Mary Pickford. Paramount Pictures later became part of that organization.

Then my parents were hit with a series of disasters in rapid succession: there was a business slump; Aubrey lost his job; his father died; and on May 10, 1927, I was born. There was nothing to do but pack up everything, including a two-week-old kid, and head back up North, but by now George Willis was dead; the farm was gone; there was no inheritance—Aubrey's share of his father's estate was a double-barreled shotgun—and there were no jobs. The stock market crash was two years in the future, but the Midwest had been economically depressed since the beginning of the 1920's. There were no safety nets of any kind. If you were out of work, you were out of luck.

My folks struggled along the best they could. Back in Marengo, a town of about 2,200 people, they found a house with rent low enough for them to manage. Even that was possible only because my mother found a job as a substitute teacher in Marengo's elementary school, which gave them a dependable, if smallish, income. The money Maude earned while my dad was out of work became a point of contention later, one that never went away. She saw to that. Depression was the first big word in my vocabulary, and broke was the first piece of slang I learned. My parents were knocked flat by circumstances, but they climbed back onto their feet, and went about making their living on an Iowa farm. General Grant is supposed to have said the last man standing after a battle is the winner. I guess he knew something about farming.

Morey

Marengo, Iowa
December 1931

After nearly five years, during which my father never held a full-time job, Maude and Aubrey decided they would give farming another try. We began to have visits from a man they called Uncle Tom, an old gentleman with a white moustache, and I learned a new word, landlord.

My mother told me stories about what it would be like to live on a farm. "You know how much you like animals? Well, on the farm there'll be chickens, and sheep, and little pigs, besides the cows and horses. You can go to the chicken house and gather eggs in a bucket. And when you're big enough, you can milk the cows."

It sounded exciting, all the different animals we would have, and how much fun it would be to feed the chickens and gather eggs. She was especially pleased about the house where we were to live.

"You know, this house we're going to live in isn't like most farm houses. This one has electric lights, and running water. What do you think about that?"

"Won't we have lamps and candles for light, and pump water from a well?" I asked.

"Well, most farmers do, but this house has lots of things farmhouses don't usually have. There's a big attic, all finished just like the other rooms in the house. You can have your own room up there. And there's an oak tree in the front yard with a platform and a tree house built in it, but you have to be very careful when you play there high up off the ground."

"Oh, yeah, I promise I'll be careful."

I would have promised anything to have a tree house all my own.

Aubrey borrowed my grandpa's Model-T Ford, and we started out to have a look at the place where we were going to live. It had rained that day, and when we turned off the paved highway a mile east of the farmhouse, we faced a clay road, all mud and deep ruts. The steep hill in front of us stopped the car dead. We couldn't move. We were stuck in the mud. This was a regular thing for people who lived on dirt roads, but it was a first time for me. We were halfway up the hill, and the old Ford couldn't, or wouldn't (there was always something personal in your dealings with a Model-T) pull itself up any further. It wouldn't go back, either. My mother's voice started to get shrill, making everything worse. My dad wasn't saying much, but what he did say sounded unfriendly. I was scared.

There were no streetlights anywhere, and it was black as the inside of a hat. Even I could see that the headlights on the Model-T were getting dim. Then, all of a sudden another car, a big one with bright lights, came over the hill toward us. The deep ruts in the road made it impossible for the cars to pass by each other. The driver stopped and got out.

"Why, that's Maury Hartz." My mother sounded like she was ready to cry.

The Hartzes were our new neighbors. Their house was a quarter-mile west of the farm where we were moving.

Maury put my mother and me into his car while he helped get the old Ford back to the paved highway. The headlights on my grandpa's Ford had gone out completely, but I had a little flashlight with me that night, shaped like a lantern. Maury took it and set it one the fender of the Model- T. I can still see that dim light moving away from us, as Maude kept saying, "Look at that boy push. Just look at that boy push."

I never did get to see the farmhouse my mother had described so enthusiastically. Later that winter, on a Saturday night when the tenants living there were in town, the house caught fire and burned to the ground. We were moving to the farm all right, but the old house (that's the way my mother always referred to it) was gone forever. A new house was immediately put up in its place, except this one didn't have running water or electric lights. I guess Uncle Tom didn't feel he could afford to reinstall those luxuries in a house where he never expected to live.

Move to the Farm
March 1, 1933

Uncle Tom's farm was four miles outside of Marengo, which is on US Highway 6, a transcontinental road that was paired with #30, the Lincoln Highway, as one of the two main roads across the country before the Interstate system. The town is 100 miles east of Des Moines, and 8 miles west of the Amana Colonies and is the County Seat of Iowa County. Aubrey signed a contract to farm on shares, which meant our rent would be half of everything we took in. Uncle Tom furnished the land, the livestock and the farm machinery, such as it was. We were literally and truly sharecroppers, although we never, ever said that about ourselves. Our situation improved later in the 1930s when Aubrey changed over to a different contract, one with a fixed rent, and some time after World War II he got around to buying the farm. I was never told how much he paid for it.

When Aubrey moved to his uncle's farm, he was thirty-five years old and he took on a job where he would have to work day and night if he was to make a go of it. I don't know how he felt about what he was undertaking, but he didn't have much choice. During the Depression you couldn't buy a job. Now he had an opportunity on his uncle's farm, not a very good opportunity, to be sure, but what else was there for him to do? Maybe he was glad to get back to farming, something he knew how to do.

The new house was built on the same foundation where the old house burned. It was only a story and a half high, but it was pretty, painted white with green-shingle siding on the second story. There was no attic, only a crawl space and some tiny cubbyholes under the eaves. Forty years later when my parents sold out and moved to town, that house was the main attraction for the people who bought the place, but my mother hated it. It wasn't the old house, and it never would be. She found fault with every door, window, wall, and stairway in the new place. A carpenter named Von Lienen built the house. Poor man, I doubt he rests easy in his grave, because my mother damned him every day of her life on the farm.

On the first day I saw our new home, I found a boy a year or two older than me riding a black horse around in the yard. I had never sat on a horse in my life, and I wanted to try it.

"Can I ride the pony?" I asked.

The yard was full of neighbors helping us move in, and getting the other family moved out. Somebody said, "Why, I guess Johnnie won't care if you ride Beauty for a while." The kid slid off his horse, and ran into the house.

Whoever it was boosted me up, and handed me the reins. There was no saddle. "Now, just pull on the side where you want her to turn. Don't worry. She's quiet."

Quiet was no word for that poor old horse. Half dead would have been a better description, but I didn't know anything about horses that day.

"Giddyap, Beauty."

The old horse didn't move. "Kick her with your heels," somebody advised.

My short legs stuck straight out, and kicking the horse with my heels didn't seem much of an option. Then one of the neighbors slapped her on the rump, and Beauty very deliberately began to put one slow foot in front of the other. We went meandering around in the yard, out to the road and back again. I felt I was getting the hang of it, enjoying being in control of things when Aubrey appeared, and started to speak to me in a low voice, as if he didn't want anyone else to hear him.

"Dick, that other boy is in the house crying because you took his pony away from him. Today is the last time he'll have a chance to ride Beauty. You're going to have to get off the horse." It was a surprise to me. I didn't know I was doing anything wrong.

Aubrey caught me as I slid off the old pony. "There's lots of stuff over in the middle yard. Go play there."

I wandered over to where a couple of men were standing beside a funny-looking machine.

"What's this for?"

One of the men squinted down at me, grinning, "Well, it looks like you're getting started right off learning what farming is all about. This here is a disc. You use a disc to chop up the clods after you plow."

The man speaking was Earl Gode. He was to be my best friend on the farm.

I started to climb up on the metal seat of the disc. Earl picked me up, and set me on it. "Now, you want to be careful, Old Timer, those discs are sharp. Don't cut yourself fooling around there." Earl called me Old Timer as long as he lived. I thought that was just great.

Well, okay, I had found the disc. What I really wanted to see was the tractor. I yanked on my new friend's sleeve. "Where's the tractor?"

He looked at me and laughed. "The tractor? Why, there ain't any tractor. You're going to work with horses here. Don't you like horses?"

I didn't know whether I did or not. Later I heard old Charlie Geisking quote a couple of lines of doggerel:

Some folks say there ain't no Hell.
They never farmed, and they can't tell.

We had the same sources of power that farmers had relied on since the beginning of time—wind and muscle. A windmill on a rise east of the barn pumped our water, and the muscles of horses and men (later add a boy) did all the rest.

The moment I discovered there was no tractor, I knew farming wasn't for me. Five years later, in 1938, Aubrey bought a big, new, bright orange Allis-Chalmers, but it was too late as far as I was concerned. I spent the next twelve years of my life planning and scheming ways to get away from the farm.

The Aurora Schoolhouse, Washington Township, Iowa County, Iowa, c.1953

Country School
March 1933

"Dick's been here at home almost three weeks now. I think you should get him back in school before the year ends."

This was Uncle Tom telling my mother he thought someone should be attending to my schooling. Giving advice like that to Maude was a risky business, but he was our landlord, and so he had the advantage of position.

"Well, I suppose so, but I've had too much on my hands to take him over there, and get him started. He's not bothering me here."

"Well, I'll show him the way he'll have to take walking to school, and I'll introduce him to Miss Nelson. It's noon now. There's time enough for us to go after we eat."

I didn't dislike the idea of going to school, but the news that I was on my way that very day, and to an entirely new kind of school at that, didn't leave me on the pinnacle of anticipation. I had been hanging around the house having a good time for myself doing nothing, and I liked that. Clearly my idleness made Uncle Tom nervous.

He took me by the hand and showed me the way across the fields, over the fences and ditches, a little less than a mile to what was to be my school for the next seven years. Uncle Tom was close to seventy, but he was still spry, and we went along in great style as he boosted me over the fences and ditches.

We started from our kitchen garden, going out through a rickety old metal gate and over a low hill north of our house. I made it a ritual to turn back at the top of the hill, and wave good-by to my mother as she watched from the kitchen window. We never failed to do it. Years later, when Maude took up painting in the manner of Grandma Moses, she attempted a view from the house with me waving good-by, but distance and the laws of perspective defeated her. In her painting, I showed up as a tiny dot lost in the middle of the field.

A guidepost on the way to our plot of timber was a faint circular indentation in the grassy slope where the capstan of a horse-powered sawmill had once stood. I imagined it was a fairy ring until Mary Howlett, a neighbor who was in the eighth grade, my guide and protector for the few weeks remaining in the school year, told me it was a track made by a horse walking around in a circle in the mud. Mary wasn't much for fantasy.

Over the open field, into the timber, and down through the trees, we came to a spot where I had to teeter my way across a shallow brook on stepping-stones. From there the path led me to the top of a bluff, then turned and ran straight north along a fence as far as the boundary of our farm. If I looked down to my left, I could see the little brook running in the same direction until it joined Hilton Creek, a stream we called the big creek. Years of spring rains and melting snow had carried stones down the ravine forming a deep gravel deposit. I called that spot the rapids. It was a fine place to pick up pretty rocks and skipping stones. It also tempted me to waste time, making me tardy at school, or home late for chores.

A big butternut tree served as a corner post for the fences where three farms came together, presenting me with two fences to clamber through. My grandpa, always at pains to smooth a path for me, sliced open a couple of three-foot lengths of garden hose, and fastened them over the barbs on the top strands of wire. Then he propped the fence up with a forked stick so that it wouldn't break down when I climbed over. His improvised stile was there for years after I graduated from country school. I never understood why seeing it made me feel sad.

When we reached US Highway 6, I could see the school less than a quarter of a mile away across Hilton Creek. There weren't many cars on the highway, but for safety's sake, we walked on the left, facing what traffic there might be. We went up a cinder path on a steep, high bank to a small white building with the word "Aurora" painted over the front door. I couldn't read, but Uncle Tom pronounced it for me, and told me that it meant sunrise. He knocked at the door, and I met my new teacher. She looked little, even to me.

"Miss Nelson, I'm Tom Willis. My son, Hugh, went to school here some years ago, a bit before your time, I think."

"Oh, yes, I know of Hugh. He's made quite a success in the

world, hasn't he?" (At that time, Hugh was vice president of Sperry Gyroscope).

Uncle Tom seemed pleased with what Miss Nelson had said. "Well, yes, he has, thank you, and now we've got another member of the family to put in your charge." He pushed me up front and center.

"This young fellow's name is Dick. He's my nephew's boy, and he'll be six years old in May. They have just moved onto my farm over south of here. Howlett's live right down the hill from them, you know, and I think Dick's mother would like it if Mary could walk home with him after school today."

"Oh, I'm sure Mary will be glad to do that. You just leave Dick here with us. We'll take good care of him."

Whatever it was that was going to happen to me was beyond my control—a feeling much like being wheeled away to surgery, I later learned.

Uncle Tom nodded and smiled. He seemed so relieved that he almost skipped as he went down the steep bank in front of the school. I didn't feel so great about it myself, but there was no way out. I was going to school in this building with this teacher.

Miss Nelson turned to me. "Now, Dick, you come inside, and I'll introduce you to the other pupils. Would you rather be called Dick, or Richard?"

"Dick, please."

In I went, about to start in a new kind of school, much different from the one I attended in town.

The interior at Aurora was arranged according to an old-fashioned requirement for country schools in our district. The floor slanted up steeply from the front of the room to the rear, where a narrow platform ran the width of the building. Facing down the slope toward the teacher's desk in front were different-sized desks to accommodate different-sized pupils. I guess the slanted floor gave the teacher a better view of everything that was going on.

Miss Nelson had been teaching at Aurora for sixteen years when I started there. The average wage for a teacher in an Iowa County rural school at that time was $55 a month, a good deal up from the $18 a month my mother had earned in 1918 when she taught at a country school called Oak Grove, west of Marengo.

Miss Nelson lived in town with her widowed mother. She walked three miles to school every morning, and back at night. Now and then somebody gave her a lift, but she never hitchhiked, always walking on the left side of the road facing the oncoming traffic.

Miss Nelson braided her light brown hair, and arranged it around her head in a kind of a crown. She wore smocks to protect her dresses from chalk and dust. In one pocket she had a gold locket watch on a chain, and she carried a little silver automatic pencil on a chain around her neck that she used to correct our schoolwork, very precisely, in red. She had a habit of looping the chain around one of her fingers and running her hand up and down the chain when she was preoccupied.

I never heard Miss Nelson raise her voice, but her moral authority was such that none of the big boys, some of whom were twice her size, ever made any kind of trouble. Times had changed, to be sure, but all of us heard stories of how in the old days bullying fellows made it a game to run off timid new schoolteachers. Nobody ever tried anything of that kind with Miss Nelson. I heard about farmers who told their boys (never their girls), "If you're whipped at school, I'll whip you again when you get home," and in those days, whip meant whip. It may have been that autocratic fathers were afraid the teacher would somehow usurp their authority. Miss Nelson never whipped anyone, but the story cropped up so often that I assume it must have had some basis in fact—at other schools, perhaps, or with other teachers.

The school yard at Aurora was roomy, an acre or two, with lots of nice trees: oak, linden, elm, box elder (those were not so nice, crawling with smelly black and red bugs), and a pair of evergreens stood on either side of a walk leading to the school. They were called cryptomeria because they were frequently found in cemeteries. In spite of that, farmers often planted them on either side of the front door. Today a forlorn pair of evergreens may be the only evidence that there was once a farmhouse on that spot.

In the northeast corner of the schoolyard, four linden trees grew from one root. They were good-sized trees, too, and we called the clump, logically, the Four Trees. They were a curiosity, our very own landmark. A few years later, when one of them blew down in a storm, they were still the Four Trees to us. At the opposite end of the lot, and nearer the center, another big linden served as home for games of hide-and-seek. Two teeter-totters and a softball bat, too heavy for any but the older boys to swing, made up the rest of our playground equipment.

Our school was heated by a big, jacketed stove placed a little off-center in the room. Midwest winter temperatures dropped to twenty, sometimes thirty, degrees below zero. A teacher's quality was sternly tested when it came time to bank the fire so that it would hold overnight. Only a real veteran could keep a fire going over the weekend. When the fire burned out, as it often did, kids coming to school after a freezing walk of a mile or two found the place icy cold. While the room warmed up—it seemed to take forever—the youngest of us sat with our feet up on a railing around the base of the stove, but older pupils had to endure (proudly) the chill at their desks. Ink froze solid, and all work had to be done in pencil until the schoolroom warmed up.

Behind the main school building was a small fuel shed. The space heater for the school burned both wood and coal. Most of the time our fuel was wood, because it was less expensive. Farmers in the district could make up all or part of their school tax with a contribution from their wood lots. It was something they resorted to when times were hard, and, in the years before World War II, times were pretty much always hard on the farm. A separate bin in the fuel shed held a supply of cobs, bright and fresh from the corn sheller. Clean corncobs made excellent kindling for starting fires in the space heater. The big boys helped by carrying buckets of coal or armloads of wood into the schoolhouse. You knew you were pretty nearly a man when your turn came to do some of the heavy work.

Sanitary arrangements were primitive. Two outdoor privies were set at the edge of the schoolyard. They smelled bad. The older boys told me that if you carried any food into a privy (I couldn't imagine why anyone would want to do that) it would be poisoned.

Regular toilet paper was a luxury our school district couldn't afford. We made do with discarded mail order catalogs, the softer index pages much preferred over the stiff coated-paper pages. One of our neighbors stocked his privy with a crock full of clean corncobs instead of paper—I am not making this up—but things were never that bad at school.

The one door to the school was at the end of the building under the belfry. An iron key for the front door looked big enough to unlock a castle. Inside, a hallway ran the width of the building, with cloakrooms at each end, one for boys and one for girls. The cloakrooms weren't really rooms at all, only areas partitioned off from the rest of the schoolroom. Hooks were set at two levels on the cloakroom walls. Kids ranging from primary to eighth grade hung up their wraps there. A shelf ran along one wall for lunch buckets. The cloakrooms smelled of overshoes, wet wool, lunchboxes with half-eaten bananas and apples, and kids who bathed pretty much once a week.

In the front hall, at one side of the entrance, there was a bench with a washbasin and a teakettle, along with a soap dish and a roller towel, later replaced with a stack of more sanitary paper towels. Unheated water came from the pump outside. Like the water on our farm, it was flinty-hard. No soap would lather in it. Just the same, in the name of cleanliness, we lined up out there before lunch every day to do what could be done with cold water and the scum from our nearly useless soap. I can't say we got ourselves shiny clean, but, as my grandma would have put it, we took the worst off.

From the belfry over the front door, the school bell called us to our lessons in the morning, and brought us in from recess and after lunch each day. A rope bell-pull came down into the hallway through a little hole in the ceiling. Everybody wanted to ring the bell, a privilege the teacher very carefully doled out only to the deserving. Miss Nelson showed us just how much pull we needed to exert on the rope to ring the bell in the familiar, cheerful ding-dong pattern. Then, in what we later knew to be an eerie foreshadowing, she added, "You mustn't toll the bell. That sounds as if there's going to be a funeral."

All our school supplies—paste and colored paper—were kept in a tall standing cabinet off to one side at the front of the room. When money for supplies was short, we made our own paste out of flour and water. You can make a pretty good paste if you cook it a while, and add a drop or so of carbolic to keep it from spoiling, but we weren't that sophisticated. We used cold water and flour, mixing up a dab at a time in jar lids, and applying it with toothpicks. It was messy stuff to work with, leaving white smears if we were careless. I didn't like to hand in anything looking smeary, and I contrived most of the time to have paste purchased from the store in town. Recalling the smell of flour and water paste gone sour takes me straight back to country school. At the front of the schoolroom, between doors to the cloakrooms, there was a semi-circular platform about six inches high. On it stood the teacher's desk, backed by a blackboard. The desk was oak with a raised section in the center angled to serve as a writing surface. The lid was hinged, and could be locked, keeping grade books and tests out of the hands of the desperados in the teacher's charge.

At Christmas time, we moved the desk away, and performed our Christmas programs on the platform at the front of the room. Its semi-circular shape gave us problems when we needed a curtain, which was made of thin muslin in vertical red and black panels. It hung from a wire above the front of the platform. We opened it to reveal our dialogs, the dramatized bits we performed, or when we sang our songs, or spoke our pieces.

Programs at Christmas, and when school closed for summer vacation, included potluck meals. Old Mr. Swain, who lived in a farmhouse behind the school, himself as white-haired and ruddy as Santa Claus, chortled, "We'd come here every day for a feast like this."

Aubrey never came to any school event, and Maude hated potlucks, afraid she would have to eat something not prepared to her standards. It was a circus to watch her picking her way through the stuff laid out for us.

About the first week of December each of us was given a sheet of one hundred Christmas seals, a different design every year, to sell in support of the national campaign fighting tuberculosis. They sold for a penny apiece.

When we returned with a dollar (or, if we had been unlucky, with some change and the unsold seals), we were given a little pin showing we'd joined in the effort to eliminate TB. You only got the pin if you sold all hundred stamps. It sounds far-fetched today, but back then we had to look around pretty carefully, even among family and close friends, to find anyone both willing and able to lay out their pennies for Christmas seals. I heard of kids who sold their whole dollar's worth to one person, but I never met a high roller like that.

Every year, we had an outbreak of one or another of what were called childhood diseases—measles, mumps, chicken pox, whooping cough or scarlet fever, ailments that went through school kids like fire through dry straw. Having been a country-school teacher, my mother had considerable knowledge of such matters. At the first sign we were about to be infested, she collected my books and kept me at home until the disease had worked its way through the school. I was spared the childhood illnesses in country school—and got all of them later when I went to high school in town.

The schoolroom was floored with white pine, oiled rather than varnished. Teachers did their own janitor work, using sweeping compound, a mixture of sand, sawdust and some kind of reddish oily fiber with a pungent smell to keep the dust down when the room was swept, but no teacher had to do any heavy work if she chose not to. Everyone was anxious to help out. It was a double winner, polishing the apple and avoiding lessons at the same time.

High up on the walls at the sides of the room hung two kerosene lamps in swinging brackets with reflectors, one on each side of the room. They must have been put there years back when the school building was used as a Grange Hall. I never saw them lighted. Daylight illuminated the interior, coming from six windows, three on each side of the room, with green roller shades, and white café curtains over the lower half of the windows. Now and then when the day was dark, too dark to read at our desks, the teacher dismissed everyone and sent us all home. It didn't happen often.

There were no screens on the door and windows, and when the weather was warm, flies and stinking box elder bugs were nuisances. Box elder bugs gave off a sickening banana smell when you stepped on them.

We were called forward to a large table for our recitations, even when there was only one pupil to answer the call. Miss Nelson liked to refer to her primary class as the little folk. It pained me to be identified as one of "the little folk."

In a one-room school, everybody hears all the recitations. I learned by ear, and, for that reason, schoolwork was easy for me. After hearing the classes ahead of me recite, I had the material already learned. That gave me extra time for the outside reading I wanted to do. It seemed to be an advantage at first, but later I turned into a lazy, often an idle, student. Lessons were easy. Why make hard work of them?

Word recognition or some similar nonsense was used to teach

reading in the schools in town, but Miss Nelson was old-fashioned, or so it seemed at the time, and she taught us to read using phonics. From bundles of flash cards, we learned the sounds of letters singly and in combinations. We learned to "sound out" words we didn't know.

Later, we were taught how to use a dictionary to get sounds and accents right, but until then some of the mistakes we made were howlers. I asked my mother what a privy ledge was after hearing Miss Nelson's meticulous pronunciation of "privilege" during a spelling drill.

Spelling lessons started in first grade. We began with five words: it, is, and, go, see. Those were fine. I had no trouble with them. Then they threw in ringers like eight, and plough, and my spelling never recovered.

Learning to read with phonics is a great way to open the doors to an education. Once started, you can go forward as fast as you want, limited only by your energy and interests. When we finished our assignments, we could read any hard-covered books we liked from home or from the library in town, and I read everything I could get my hands on.

In the school year 1935-36, the two oldest boys in school were Billy Spurrier and Charlie Ritchie, both about thirteen. Next oldest were Ernest Bell and Bob Schumacher. They were probably ten. Then came the largest grade in school: Hazel Schumacher, Betty Lou Olsen, Wilda Ritchie, and me—all of us around eight years old. Ruth Schumacher must have been six, and Freeman (Fritz) Ritchie, the smallest of us, was just five. We were all present in the one snapshot I have of us. We never had more than eight pupils at Aurora, nor did we ever have all eight grades at one time.

When they introduced me to fractions in the fourth grade, I was lost. No one explained the principal terms, numerator and denominator, and I struggled unhappily until the teacher told me, perhaps in desperation, "Now don't you worry any more about it. One of these days, this will all come clear to you, and you'll wonder why it ever seemed so difficult." I don't know what the Educationists would think of her approach, but it turned out she was right.

When temperatures dropped below zero, my mother often kept me at home. During the terrible winter of 1935-36, I stayed home for six weeks straight. I had my books, and presumably I was keeping up with the assignments. Everybody thought that was a good idea, because my mother had once been a teacher. Let me tell you, the experience gave me a clear understanding of why doctors don't treat their own families. I was a champion procrastinator; Maude was an inveterate nag. Together we were a disastrous combination. Aurora didn't offer courses in family relations.

Maude was a great believer in the healing powers of Nature. In her view, fresh air and sunshine would cure just about anything. I suffered from terrible colds when I was a kid, discovering years afterward that I had chronic bronchitis. On clear, frigid days my mother would bundle me off to school saying, "Now breathe deep. Let that good, clean air wash out your lungs." Breathing deep in those sub-zero temperatures was about the same as inhaling broken glass. When I came into a warm room, I coughed like a seal, but nothing ever shook Maude's faith in the curative properties of cold fresh air.

We used hand signals to get permission to move around the schoolroom. If you wanted to ask the teacher a question, you raised your full hand; three fingers let you go get a book; two fingers were raised for permission to speak to another pupil; and—the big one—one finger was raised for permission to go to the privy. The response to that request was inevitably, "Is it necessary?" Now, tell me, did any kid ever say it wasn't?

One day, a girl standing at the blackboard at the back of the room, on the high end of the slanting floor, wet her pants. Why she didn't raise her hand for permission to leave the room, I still don't understand. Maybe she thought it was all too complicated. Her prolonged indecision resulted in a golden stream running downhill to the front of the room, to the great amusement of everyone except the red-faced victim.

Ernie Bell had a rough time in school. Ernie wasn't slow, he was a whiz at anything to do with electronics, but he hated school, and he spent his time daydreaming and looking out the window. Every teacher we had nagged at him: "Ernest! Do you have all your work done? Get to work now, Ernest. Stop looking out the window." I hope whatever Ernie saw outside was interesting. He paid a high enough price for it.

My walks back and forth to school taught me about the outdoors.

I loved the sounds—water running over stones, and birdcalls. Maude taught me to identify a few of her favorites, and to listen to their songs: cardinals in winter, orioles in summer, and robins in spring. The strong, melodious call of meadow larks soared over the hay fields and pastures in summer, a sound now almost entirely vanished, as changed methods of farming have destroyed the larks' nesting places.

The melancholy whistle of phoebes, calling as if to a lost sweetheart, was a first sign of spring. They began to sing while late winter snow was still on the ground. Robins were my mother's favorite. Mine was the catbird. They would imitate anything they heard. I used to tease them into copying a few notes whistled for them. Crows seemed to have their own harsh, intelligent chatter as they gathered in their societies to forage, and for mutual protection. Farmers said crows could tell the difference between a man carrying a long stick and one who was carrying a gun.

Each season had its own special sounds: wind whispering among green leaves or shrieking through bare branches. With a violent summer storm on its way, what is scarier than the distant rumble of thunder? Then the whole sky changed to a greenish-black. The look of the clouds gave me a twist in the pit of my stomach. Summer rain showers drenched me in downpours I could never outrun.

In the spring of the year, our timber was covered with the yellow-gold lace of buds starting to emerge. Later, mild summer winds sent puffs of clouds racing across our pastures, building up waves rolling endlessly across fields ankle-deep in grass. White clover blossoms turned the pasture snowy white, and filled the air with a fragrance that made my head spin. Bluebirds, their breasts bright orange, flashed past great clumps of wild roses beside the roads. The smell of clover blossoms mixed with the scent of cut hay, a field of ripening grain or newly tasseled corn.

When we gathered walnuts in the fall, the soft, squishy outer hulls stained my hands deep brown. The color wouldn't wash off with soap, but it cleaned up quickly if you rubbed it with a piece of green tomato. Leaves of the mullein plant we called Iowa tobacco were velvety soft to the touch, but they stung like fury if you rubbed them on your face, or, worse, on your backside when you were caught short and needed a substitute for toilet paper.

Autumn filled the air with fluff from cottonwood trees and the silver streamers of balloon spiders. Web barriers were thrown across paths by huge, scary (and harmless) yellow and black garden spiders, enough to panic me as I walked along with my head down, studying the ground and paying no attention to where I was going. Our patch of timber was a wall of brown and dull-red oak trees in fall, punctuated by splashes of red and yellow from the few hard maples. November was the iron-black Puritan month, imprinted with death, its grim look relieved by the first snow.

In good weather, walking to school was pleasant, but in winter, with a north wind blowing and the temperature fifteen or twenty degrees either side of zero, it was an ordeal. My face was tanned as brown from the winter wind as it had been from the sun. A clear line of white-to-brown was drawn on my cheeks by the edges of my leather helmet. There may have been a sharp north wind to face in the morning, but at night I was hustled along by that same wind at my back. Carrying a dinner pail shut off the circulation in my hand, so I slung my lunch bucket on a strap over my shoulder.

The first bell rang at eight o'clock as a warning. Our school day started half an hour later with a warning tap at eight twenty-five, and the last bell at eight-thirty. On a clear day, I could hear the eight o'clock bell across the fields at our house as I was leaving, but that was never enough to prevent me from dawdling along, checking out trees and flowers, or searching the brook for quartz diamonds.

You weren't counted late if you were in your seat while the bell was still ringing. I got accustomed to the sound of that tiresome bell as I came puffing up the bank from the highway, envying and hating those who managed perfect attendance.

A flagpole stood outside in front of the building, and a flag-raising ceremony started the day, at least when the weather was good. With the war coming on, raising the flag became a big deal, a two-person task assigned on a rotating basis. One carried the flag and held it while it was being raised; the other pulled the rope. The same two people brought the flag down at the end of the day, willingly staying the few extra minutes for the honor of the thing.

Where our notions of flag etiquette came from, God only knows, but somehow we learned that the flag was never to touch the ground.

I don't know what we thought would happen to us if it did, but the consequences, however vague, were dreadful. Maybe leprosy?

When the weather was bad, we said our morning Pledge of Allegiance inside facing the blackboard behind the teacher's desk where a smaller flag was pinned between portraits of Washington and Lincoln, and underscored with oversized examples of Palmer Method penmanship. Decades later the words "under God" were added to the Pledge, but we went along happily, never guessing we had risked damnation without that formula.

A country school was an excellent place to learn, if you had a talented teacher, a good supply of books and support at home. I was lucky on all counts. Maude read to me whenever she had spare time, and she saw to it that I had a card from the Marengo Library so I could read on my own. Most important of all, Miss Nelson was a superior teacher, although she never had any formal preparation beyond her high school normal courses, and a few seminars. She had a widespread reputation. Student teachers came to our school as observers because of it. We also had an enlightened County Superintendent of Schools, Alice DeSpain. She and Miss Nelson got the best they could for us with the limited resources they had at hand.

My love for reading added to the tension between Aubrey and me. He griped about my always having my nose in a book, but excelling at my studies was a way to compensate for the fact I was no good at sports.

Open bookshelves on the west wall of the room held our library. Although I think I read every book in the building, I can remember only two titles: *Huckleberry Finn*, and *The Story of a Bad Boy* by Thomas Bailey Aldrich, a great yarn. He wasn't really such a bad boy after all, as Aldrich himself said in his introduction.

Music at our school was supplied by a hand-cranked Victrola on an unused desk at the rear of the room. The records were brittle disks played at seventy-eight revolutions a minute. We handled those fragile platters as if they had been made of glass. The Victrola could be turned down to thirty-three RPM and we thought it was the funniest thing in the world to hear the words drawled out in a growling bass.

Our collection of records was nothing if not eclectic. Along with Sousa marches and the patriotic standards, we had Stephan Foster's songs, along with "The Amaryllys Waltz," "Billy Boy," "Oh, Suzanna!" "Sourwood Mountain," "Frog Went a-Courting," and sentimental pieces like "Love's Old Sweet Song, " "Bendemere's Stream" and "The Hills of Tyrol."

Today the very word penmanship sounds quaint, but we were drilled in the Palmer Method. Miss Nelson was the only person I ever met in the world who could actually write that way. Each of us had an assortment in our pencil boxes, and our day-to-day schoolwork was done with whatever we owned in the way of fountain pens or ever-sharp pencils, but we were required to do all Palmer Method exercises, the ovals and the push-pulls, using pens we dipped in ink. We hated those pens that were forced on us— straight pens, or scratch pens, or dip pens we called them, simply wooden holders for steel nibs. You may be sure we never used dip pens for anything other than the exercises required. They were wretched things, given to scratching and blotting. We hauled them out only when we were compelled to do so. According to the manual, the pen was to be held so lightly it could easily be lifted out of your fingers by the supervising teacher. In reality, we clutched our pens like grim death. If the pen was in fact mightier than the sword, we were ready to prove it on the spot.

Carrying a lunch was, at first, one of the novelties of going to a rural school. I had started school in town, where kids in kindergarten were on a half-day schedule, and where I ate my noon meal at home. When we moved to the farm, Maude bought my first dinner bucket at a store in town called the "Square D," the same place that sold schoolbooks. It was made for a little kid, shaped like a box, with a lid that flipped up, and two handles that joined together for carrying. Mostly pink with some white decorations, from the first day I saw it I couldn't wait for it to wear out. I wanted something more masculine looking, like the big boys carried, and, without actually setting out to wreck my dinner pail, I did let it swing against wire fences and trees, as much as I could. No doubt a cheap Japanese import, it lasted until the school year ended in May 1933.

The self-sufficiency of farmers is a hoary myth, however dearly it may be held by people who claim to love those distant and generally dreadful times. A glance inside our dinner pails says a good deal about how independent we really were. With the exception of milk, only a small part of what we carried for lunch came directly from the farms. In the fall, before the first killing frost spoiled them, some of us carried raw tomatoes. Pickles and apples came from home, and we often had farm-raised meat in our sandwiches. Chicken was a luxury reserved for Sunday dinner. One of President Hoover's slogans was "A chicken in every pot." They must have stayed in the pot, because they sure didn't turn up in our lunch buckets very often. Most of what was in our lunches came from the grocery store. Few people baked their own bread, and those who did used flour and yeast they bought in town.

Jell-O was a big lunch favorite—at least it was among mothers—sometimes livened with chunks of orange or banana, and carried in a glass jar with a piece of waxed paper under the screw-top lid to keep it from leaking.

Our sandwiches were made with things like processed cheese, peanut butter, lunch meats, sliced baloney, sandwich spread (mayonnaise with bits of pickle chopped up in it,) jelly—usually, but not always made at home—and, for the poorest among us, plain lard on bread with nothing at all to help it out. Things were that bad on farms in the '30s.

Cold lunches get monotonous, never mind how much love may have gone into the packing. In the supply cupboard at school we had a folding wire grill and a large, wooden-handled kitchen fork we used to toast cheese sandwiches in the space heater. We stood in front of the open stove door and held our sandwiches over the hot coal fire as it made its own contribution to the flavor. Today, a grilled cheese sandwich without an overlay of coal smoke tastes flat to me.

We also ate potatoes, which had three things going for them: they were good, they were cheap and they were available. We washed our raw potatoes clean, leaving the jackets on. On cold days with the fire going full blast, we set our potatoes on the metal jacket of the stove next to the smoke pipe. From time to time during the morning, the teacher stepped over to the stove and turned the potatoes with her fingers—another of her non-academic duties. By noon, the spuds were baked through. We cut them open, and ate them with a dab of butter and some salt and pepper, or sometimes we just ate them plain. They were a nice relief from sandwiches.

Whatever we carried to drink was likely to have been milk or a sweet beverage of some kind. Nobody said anything about what the sweet stuff might do to our teeth, but the teachers warned us often and sternly about the evils of drinking tea and coffee. The anti-coffee campaign was pretty effective. I don't think any of us drank coffee or tea until we were adults.

For outside recreation, we did our best with what we had, in spite of the fact we never had enough kids to make up two teams for a softball game. There was always a wrangle about whether or not over the fence should be out. The big boys didn't want that restriction, while the girls and smaller boys—I was one of them—knew it was the only way we had a ghost of a chance of getting up to bat.

"That's over the fence! You're out."

"No, I'm not, either. I saw you kick it through the wire."

"You're a liar! It rolled through."

"You're such a great fielder, why don't you catch a fly ball, if you want to put me out?"

Miss Nelson had each of us bring a mop handle from home to use in some kind of exercise program. Later the mop sticks were put to many uses. Italy had recently invaded Ethiopia, and one of our favorite games was the Ethiopians' defense of their homeland. Our mop handles substituted for the spears and muskets we saw in newsreels being used to fight the villainous Italians.

At the picture show in town a Paramount newsreel showed the Ethiopian Emperor, Haile Selassie, shouted down by Italian newsmen when he tried to address the League of Nations. He was a tiny little man, and he was alone. It didn't look fair. Many years later that same little man walked side by side with Charles DeGaulle, one of the tallest heads of state in the world, unguarded and unprotected, in President Kennedy's funeral procession. They may not have been well matched, but they were impressive.

US Highway 6 ran in front of our school, a two-lane road eighteen feet wide overall. Aurora was set on a high bank overlooking the road, and at noon and recesses we scrutinized everything passing by. Traffic was a fraction of what it is today, but what there was provided us with an endless source of dispute. Arguments about the supposed strong and weak points of the cars we saw took us to the brink of bloodletting.

We split into two camps—those for Ford and those for Chevrolet (we pronounced it Chivvy). Ford had just introduced a new V-8 engine that gave their cars terrific pick-up and speed. What we knew about cars was mostly plucked out of the air, but we never let mere lack of information dampen our enthusiasm. When the Chivvy gang sneered that Fords burned too much oil, those of us on the other side weren't inclined even to acknowledge such a puny attack.

The economics of farming meant there were few new-car owners among us. My folks drove a Model-T until late 1935, friends had an old Dodge touring car that had lost its folding top, another family owned a Teraplane. How could you take people seriously when they drove a car with a name like that?

We evaluated what we saw passing by on Number 6. "Look at that new V-8 there. That's my car."

"Yeah, that's your car. Your car is still hitched to a horse."

"Yeah? Well it's better than that old Model-T you've got."

"Yeah? Our Model-T will go through mud deep enough to drown that greedy Chivvy of yours."

"I'd sure like to see that. I'd sure like to see any road too bad for our Chivvy to get through."

And so it went, on and on, with never a final decision. The only car we all agreed on was the 1936 DeSoto. It was a stunner, futuristic, and a real coup for whoever spotted it first.

We were also fascinated with the Iowa State Liquor Commission trucks. Prohibition had been voted out at the start of the Roosevelt Administration, and the Commission had not had time to get trucks of its own into service, making do instead with vehicles leased from a commercial mover, White Line Transport. The danger of highjacking was real enough. Mobsters all across the country, especially in Chicago and Kansas City, reveled in their opportunities.

A guard rode shotgun beside the driver on the liquor transports. You could spot those trucks by a loophole in the windshield on the passenger side, and if you were lucky, you might catch a glimpse of the Thompson sub-machine gun the guard held in his lap.

Aurora was only yards away from the railroad tracks, and in the 1930s, when Rock Island introduced The Rocket, its first streamline diesel train, all of us agreed there wasn't much room left for improvement in transportation. We lined up in front of our school to watch the Rockets go by.

"Would you look at that?"

"I guess that'll put your old Silver Nosed Flier [a steam locomotive with the front end of its boiler painted aluminum, until then one of our favorites] out of business."

With Rock Island passenger trains in clear view only a few yards away, an itch to travel set in hard for me. I wanted nothing so much as to get away from the farm, and the sight of people eating in dining cars, snow-white table cloths with sparkling silver, and waiters serving them, affected me like strong drink. I was fiddle-footed. For me, life on the farm was life in prison.

During the Depression, men were constantly on the move in search of jobs. US 6, a transcontinental highway, ran in front of our school, right under our noses, but we didn't see much hitchhiking. Highways were not good enough, nor were cars comfortable enough, for many people to make long trips by automobile. More to the point, nobody had any money. Men down on their luck bummed rides on freight trains. Boxcars and flat cars on the Rock Island Railroad swarmed with hoboes, all sunburned and ragged, crossing the country trying to find work, and not having much luck at it, either.

Later the Civilian Conservation Corps (CCC) took up part of the slack, and as the country slowly began to gather itself together for the war everyone knew was coming, the draft scooped up unemployed men. When troops in training began to move along the highway in front of our school, we boys were constantly angling to get outside—a clear misuse of the one-finger request—to stare and to wave at the passing troop convoys, tarpaulin-covered trucks pulling howitzers, loaded with helmeted men.

One rainy evening in the spring of 1935 when I was in second grade, the telephone rang. Maude answered, and began to scream at the top of her lungs. Gradually, through my mother's hysterics, I understood that Miss Nelson had been killed on the highway. She had worked late that afternoon, the Ritchie kids and Betty Lou Olson who usually walked with her luckily had gone on ahead. It was a dark, wet day, and it seems a car traveling east—Miss Nelson was walking west, and, as she always did, she was facing the oncoming traffic—had gone out of control on a curve.

The car rolled over on its side. Only after the driver and his companion crawled out of the wreck did they see her feet sticking out from under it. Her head was crushed, and we were told she died instantly. Miss Nelson was fifty-five years old.

The driver was a doctor from Cedar Rapids. He claimed he hadn't seen her, but no one believed his story. No one felt bad about it either when, a few years later, we heard he had committed suicide.

I didn't attend Miss Nelson's funeral. Maude said I was too young.

A young woman named Helen Misel came to Aurora to finish out the year, and then taught for another year. She was an inexperienced teacher who seemed worse because she was constantly compared to Miss Nelson. Discipline fell apart, and school degenerated into a constant uproar.

The next teacher at Aurora was one of our neighbors, Wallace McLennan, a middle-aged woman who lived on a farm about a mile east of our school. Her father had given Aurora its name. Old Fred Ritchie had three kids in school, and he was outraged when he heard that a married woman might be our next teacher. He came to the farm one evening with a petition urging that she not be hired.

Fred was a tall, spare fellow from West Virginia, and he made his point to my parents in his twanging mountaineer's voice, "Now, she's a married woman. Now, her place is in the home." Mrs. McLennan had a grown daughter, married and living away from home. My folks were not won over by Fred's argument.

Wally McLennan taught at Aurora for three years. She was a good, solid teacher with a taste for wise sayings. One of her favorites ran, "Patience is a virtue. Possess it if you can. It's found seldom in a woman, and never in a man." That gem put me squarely on the side of the sexists, where I remained for a good while. Another of her maxims was, "Can't never did anything. I'll try does wonders."

When I was in the fifth grade, all pupils in Iowa County took a set of standard tests evaluating their academic progress. It turned out I was reading at the ninth-grade level. Mrs. McLennan let me know she had a great deal to do with my test scores, and she was probably right to take credit for it.

Maude explained to me that I had a choice—she let me make my own decision—of going along as I was, or of taking two grades in one year. Aubrey wasn't involved in the discussion. I grabbed at the opportunity for advancement, mostly for the notoriety that went with it. Then I discovered you can't be identified as a bright kid and still have people like you. I didn't do much to ease the situation, either, but strutted as much as the law allowed.

A pretty young woman named Kathryn Frick was my last teacher, when I was in the seventh and eighth grades. It was her family who had lived on Uncle Tom's farm when the old house burned, but we never talked about that.

Miss Frick rode a bicycle out from town when the weather was good. It was her first year of teaching, she had lots of energy, and we were all enchanted with her. She wore sweaters that fit, as they used to say, right now, a matter in which I was beginning to take some interest. I wasn't the only one. Every now and then our classes were interrupted when some young man knocked at the door of the school, and Miss Frick came back into the room smiling and blushing.

I packed up my books, and walked away from Aurora for the last time in May 1940 feeling relieved and excited. A tiny crack was beginning to appear in the walls that held me prisoner on the farm. Getting out of country school a year early meant I would graduate from high school when I was barely seventeen. It seemed to be a small matter then, but it made a big difference later.

"Alone, alone, all, all alone...."
—*The Rhyme of the Ancient Mariner*
1933–1934

I solation and solitude held us between their paws when the sun went down. After dark we looked around the horizon for our neighbors' kerosene lamps, their mellow light glowing warm and friendly in the evening gloom. At the top of the hill east a quarter of a mile was Jim Butler's place. The Howletts lived down the hill west and a little north of us. Barely visible over the hill to the west were the Hartzes' lights. At the top of a the next hill was Everett Timm's farm, and another mile west of that we could just make out the lights of the Conn place. Northwest of us, near an old cemetery, were the Kurth's lights, a farmstead now entirely vanished. A ridge cut off our view to the south. Over north two or three miles, woods and hills along the Iowa River were sprinkled with tiny dots of light from the farms there, all of them too far away for us to think of them as neighbors. And that was it.

Our roads went from bad to impassable depending on the season of the year, and darkness closed us in on ourselves. Then you could hope that the day had been pleasant, that the night might be peaceful and that you would not be caught in the middle of a family row. When that happened, there was no escape, nowhere to go and no way to get there if there had been.

You can probably imagine a time without television, when radio was the only way to get news and entertainment. Now think of what it might have been like without a radio. That was our situation during the first winter on the farm in 1933–34. Today when I hear the treacly old Christmas tunes, I think of my mother complaining that she wouldn't spend another winter cooped up on that farm with no Christmas music. Not long after that a big, floor model battery-powered radio made its appearance in our front room. It was secondhand.

A new Zenith or GE six-tube radio sold for $24.95, five cents less than Aubrey paid a hired man for a month's hard work.

Our radio used two kinds of batteries: a twelve-volt "A" battery, the same as in an automobile, and a "B" battery, sealed in a cardboard container, nearly twice the size of the A. When the A battery ran low, you could take it to a filling station or a garage to be recharged, but when the B battery ran down, there was no way around the problem. Reception got worse and worse until finally you had to buy a replacement.

A series of radio programs for kids ran every weekday evening. I raced through my barnyard chores when I got home from school so I could be in the house at 5:30 for *The Adventures of Jack Armstrong, the All-American Boy*. Jim Ameche, Don Ameche's brother, played the title role.

After *Jack Armstrong* there was *Little Orphan Annie* at 5:45. Both *Jack Armstrong* and *Little Orphan Annie* ran promotions to get kids to buy Wheaties (*Jack Armstrong*) or Ovaltine (*Little Orphan Annie*). You sent in box tops from Wheaties, or the aluminum seal— "or a reasonably accurate facsimile"—from the inside of an Ovaltine can, along with a dime or a quarter in order to receive some treasure—a magic talisman, a ring that decoded secret messages, or some other gem irresistible to a kid. They seemed to take an eternity to arrive in the mail.

At 6 o'clock everyone in the country tuned their radios to catch the notes of "The Perfect Song," the theme that introduced *Amos 'n Andy*. People had to be very busy or in the midst of a great crisis not to listen to that program. We knew from reading newspapers and magazines that two white actors played all the roles on the show, a comedy program about blacks. What difference did that make? We lived in a white community, and it was radio after all. In our imaginations, they were black.

Weekly radio shows played in half-hour segments. On Sunday, people listened to Jack Benny and his partner Mary Livingstone. Mary was truly Jack's wife, but they never mentioned that on the program. Benny's announcer, Don Wilson, his bandleader Phil Harris, and the tenor on the show, Dennis Day, were as much a part of the production as Benny himself. The fantasy feud between Jack Benny and Fred Allen was one of the best known and longest running gags on the radio.

We picked up the wisecrack, "Taint funny, McGee!" from *Fibber McGee and Molly*. Catch phrases and theme music from radio shows became part of our lives. I doubt that anyone of my generation can hear the opening notes of the "William Tell Overture" without feeling an urge to yell, "Hi-Yo, Silver!" *The Lone Ranger* owned that music.

The quality of radio reception was a function of the distance between the transmitting station and the receiving set. We almost always got good reception from station WHO, a hundred miles away in Des Moines. They had a young sportscaster there named Ronald Reagan. Everybody called him "Dutch." H.R. Gross read the evening news. Gross went to Congress as an ultraconservative member of the House of Representatives, and we all know how Reagan ended up, but in the 1930s, if anyone had said Dutch Reagan was going to be president of the United States, I'm pretty sure he'd have been hooted out of the county.

Radio station WMT was only thirty miles away in Cedar Rapids. We could depend on hearing it loud and clear. The Cedar Valley Hill-Billies was a popular group at WMT, sponsored by Jolly Jack Jaeger. Jolly Jack owned a second-floor department store in Cedar Rapids. He was an irrepressible fellow who loved getting on the air to tell us all, in his thick German accent, "Jaeger's moved up to bring prices down!" Jaeger's moved up for the same reason Chinese restaurants move up; the higher you went, the lower the rent.

We had pretty good reception from WGN in Chicago, but it was usually impossible to get the other big Chicago station, WMAQ, on the Mutual Network. Reception was always bad, and we didn't hear Orson Welles' Martian invasion program, *War of the Worlds*, when it was first broadcast. It is a fair measure of our isolation that, when at last we did hear Welles' program, it seemed to have happened in another country.

Our connection with our neighbors was by telephone. Almost every farm had a phone, although the place east of us did not. People living there walked down to our house when they wanted to make a phone call. My mother took this as an imposition, and she made no bones about letting everyone know how she felt. Maude was ready to help most people when she thought they were in need, even if she had to kill them to do it, but she could be selective with her barbwire largess.

Our telephone line was a single-wire system, called a non-metallic line, grounded in the earth rather than by a return wire. With several parties on such a system, the signal weakened when neighbors picked up their telephone receivers to listen, making it nearly impossible for the people phoning to hear each other. Then the principal parties had to stop and ask the interlopers to hang up—which may or may not have worked—depending on the subject under discussion, and how anxious the neighbors were to snoop.

Farm telephones were big, clumsy oak boxes mounted on the wall. The transmitter stuck out from the body of the phone like a goose's neck, and the receiver hung on a hook at the side of the instrument. You turned a hand crank on the phone in order to reach "Central," two or three operators at Marengo's privately owned telephone exchange. We were acquainted with all the women who worked there. There were no male telephone operators. The story was that men had once been tried for those positions, but they turned out to be too sassy.

There were advantages in having an acquaintance at the central exchange. In 1944, one of my friends, Armand Terpening from Army language school, passing through Marengo on a furlough, tried to call my grandparents. Gertie Freeze, the operator on duty that day, lived a half a block from my grandma. She broke in to tell my friend, "Dick's grandma is shopping in Cedar Rapids. She won't be home today."

Each family on the party line had its own ring that identified incoming calls. The ring for our farm was two longs and two shorts. Down the road, the Hartz family ring was a short and a long. Timm's ring was two longs, and so on through the neighborhood. We heard all the different rings as they came through. It was easy to tell the difference between calls cranked in by a neighbor compared to those from Central in town. Rings from Central were strong and firm, while those from a hand crank had a weak, uncertain quality about them.

Long-distance calls also had especially strong rings. They were easy to identify, and they always meant bad news. No one made an expensive long-distance call to pass on a good word. I still flinch when I know someone is calling me long distance, just as I reflexively shout into the telephone on a long-distance call, unconvinced that anyone in California can hear me if I speak in a normal tone from New York.

When the phone rang, no matter for whom it was intended, it was a great temptation for lonely men and women on the farms to pick up the receiver and listen. My mother would never admit she did it, but she always seemed to know what was going on in the neighborhood. What there was to hear was mostly pretty flat. Only now and then some love-struck pair threw all caution to the light breezes of our underdeveloped technology, sighing and gulping their hearts' desires to the flapping ears of half the township.

About ten o'clock in the morning on week days a "line call" came from Central with the weather forecast and the market reports for the day, the current prices of grain and meat and the numbers of hogs, cattle and sheep that had been sold the day before in Chicago. A line call was ten short rings followed by one long ring. The same signal was used to bring help in case of an emergency—a fire or an injury. A line call was the one time when we were supposed to pick up the phone and listen.

We didn't do much socializing on the farm. People met and gossiped in town on Saturday night, the big night out for farmers, but it didn't go much beyond that. Everyone complained that no one "neighbored" anymore. Someone might come by to talk business, and stay for an hour or so, but that was about all there was to it. Those impromptu visits were a high point for me. I loved having people around, and never got enough of it—and for good reason. It almost never happened.

Drinking played no part in polite get-togethers. Alcohol was refused or abused, for the most part. No respectable woman drank in public. A woman seen drinking in a tavern might as well have gone out with a mattress on her back. We lived in a mainly Protestant, puritanical society where drinking was regarded as a bad thing. There were few exceptions.

Our real social life came when everyone worked together making hay, thrashing or filling silos. Then we pulled together in a common purpose, with a feeling of neighborliness, of sharing something important. The work was hard, but with everyone taking part, it was pleasant. Then neighboring meant something.

At harvest some farmers eased the rules a little, treating the crew to bottles of beer buried in ice in a metal silage basket. Everybody had one. Kids might get a sip if they were standing near some generous soul.

Jim Butler was our neighborhood drunk. There were others who drank heavily, but Jim was out and away the worst. He lived alone on the farm east of us, trying to make a living on the kind of land Ethan Frome might have farmed, eighty acres of steep, yellow-clay hills, a prime setting for failure. Most of Jim's neighbors were afraid of him. He was a tall man with chiseled features, jet-black hair and a swarthy complexion. I thought he must look like Injun Joe in Tom Sawyer. It seems to me that Jim had a bass-baritone voice, although that's odd because I can't recall ever hearing him speak.

Jim Butler had been married, but his wife was dead. She had been a teacher, and Jim brought me a box full of her books, among them *Hans Brinker, or the Silver Skates*, and a small, leather-bound volume, *The Vision of Sir Launfal*. I still have it, although it is now falling apart. My mother read aloud to me from those books, but she hated history, and she skipped the chapters in Hans Brinker (roughly every other one) that dealt with the history of Holland.

Jim was viciously abusive to his livestock when he was drunk. He hitched a pair of old plugs to an ancient spring wagon when he wanted to go to town. Falling-down drunk by the time he was ready to come home, he beat his skinny team every step of the way back.

One day, Jim tried to take a sow into town to market, driving her on foot, guiding her with a stick he was carrying. Pigs are at least as intelligent as dogs, and they are ornery, cross-grained animals when they want to be. By the time Jim got his sow as far as our place, she was bleeding from her mouth and eyes, and he had given up on the idea of getting her to town. The sow died in our barnyard the next day.

Aubrey had one encounter with Jim Butler that made him nervous. It was a winter evening, already dark, and the old man was alone in the barn doing the milking. People accustomed to electric lights forget how dark it was in a barn lighted only with a kerosene lantern.

Getting into our barn and back to where the cows stood locked in their stanchions involved opening a sliding door on a squeaky track, and then getting through a runway full of beef cattle. Jim somehow managed to make his way back to where Aubrey was milking. When Aubrey looked up, he saw Jim standing right next to him in the dim lantern light, weaving like a tree in the wind. The old man was so startled he forgot his manners altogether, just invited Jim to get the hell out of there. He was never really cordial to Jim Butler after that.

The day came when Jim was found dead in a ditch. He had been on his way home after a spree. His sad old team was there on the road beside him, their heads drooping, waiting for him to get up and beat them. This time they didn't have to worry.

People who lived alone, unable to get out, suffered a good deal in their isolation. Mrs. Conn lived two miles west of us. She was older than my parents, and a great friend of my grandmother's. Her husband was long dead, and her son, Rex, didn't pay much attention to her; and the poor old lady was starved for company.

We stopped for some reason at Conn's farm one Saturday night about seven o'clock on our way to town to do the week's shopping. Mrs. Conn was quite stout. She moved around only with great effort, but she talked the entire time we were there, never pausing, rolling her bulk back and forth on the sofa where she was sitting, gasping for breath between words. She seemed afraid that if she stopped talking we might go away and leave her alone.

I wanted to go on to town, but I could see that my parents didn't know how to get out the door. Mrs. Conn's enjoyment of our visit was so pathetic that they were ready to put up with anything in order not to hurt her feelings. I was a silent minority sulking at the edge of the problem.

Minutes and hours ticked away. Mrs. Conn talked on and on. Ten o'clock came and went, and when Maude and Aubrey at last scraped up their courage to break away, it was approaching midnight, far too late to go to town. Politely, if gloomily, we turned around and went home.

Farmers living a long way from their neighbors, with roads often impassable, dreaded fire most of all. The house we lived in replaced one that had burned to the ground shortly before we moved to the farm. There was no wind that night; the windmill wasn't turning. Water to put out the fire had to be pumped from an open well in the barnyard. In the confusion, nobody remembered to put water into the cooling system of the old gasoline one-lunger on the pump. The engine overheated so badly it never ran properly again.

The barn caught fire, too, and was extinguished only by strenuous efforts of a bucket brigade, neighbors who had come to watch the house burn down. Aubrey was there helping put out the fire that spread to the barn. He carried a scar on his head where he was hit by a carelessly passed bucket, and he never tired of pointing out the charred rafters in the haymow.

There was some mystery around those events. People whispered that it might have been an "insurance fire." How did the house catch fire in the first place with the entire family in town? On a windless evening, how could sparks from the burning house have got into the hayloft? Those questions were never answered. People in the neighborhood argue about it to this day.

If a kerosene lamp were dropped, a minor accident could easily turn into a catastrophe. Most lamps were made of glass or china, and a dropped lamp became a Molotov cocktail (a term we had not yet learned). The resulting fire would almost certainly destroy the house before help arrived. It was a mark of extra responsibility, and I felt especially puffed up when I was given a lamp to carry.

Isolation was a major factor in farm disasters. Maude nearly burned our house down on one occasion when she was working alone, cleaning Iowa-coal clinkers out of the furnace. Having got as far as she could with the job for the moment, she hung the poker on a wall covered with tarpaper without thinking that the poker had been sitting in hot coals in the furnace for some time.

Somebody had tacked a mesh bag of black walnuts up to dry alongside the nail where she hung the poker. Maude was attending to other chores in the next room when she heard a sound like corn popping. The hot poker ignited the tarpaper wall, and the fire burned through the sack of walnuts. The corn-popping sound that attracted her attention in this House-that-Jack-Built sequence came from walnuts dropping onto the cement floor.

Maude dashed upstairs to phone our nearest neighbor a quarter of a mile away, and then hustled back down into the basement to fight the fire on her own. Call it brave, call it foolish, she was determined not to let the house burn down. The fact she had started the fire herself may have given her some extra motivation.

In the room next to the furnace there was a hand pump connected to a cistern holding soft rainwater used for laundry. The wall beside the furnace was blazing as she pumped bucket after bucket of water, throwing it on the flames.

She had the fire out, and was gasping for breath, when the unflappable neighbor she called earlier appeared at the back door wanting to know if she could use any help. His name was Vern Fergusson, and from that day forward my mother never left off telling the world what a slowpoke he was.

We hadn't had a drop of rain for months, and next day, when Maude started to pump water from the cistern to do a washing, she found the tank was dry. Those last few gallons of rainwater, and her determination, had saved the house.

Belly Acres
Early 1930s

My mother was great with wisecracks. She called our new home Belly Acres. Maude made a lot of sour jokes about the place where we lived, and for good reason. Everything on our farm, and I mean every single thing, had to be repaired before it could be used. Aubrey was able to turn his hand to just about any task. His guiding principle was "not much for looks but hell for stout."

All the buildings needed paint. Worse, several were simply falling down, including a corncrib, a granary, a machine shed and a chicken house. Hundreds of yards of fence needed repair. There wasn't a single decent set of harness on the place. Aubrey cobbled something workable together out of the bits and pieces he had on hand. Even the lines—the reins—had to be made up from scraps he spliced together. Rundown machinery and the sad state of our horses made the hard job of farming that much worse.

We had five head of horses with three good eyes among them. Queen, the best mare, could see with both eyes. A little mare we called Babe was blind in one eye. The rest were stone blind, all of them.

We could only guess how old our horses were. When a horse passes the age of twelve, you can no longer tell its age by looking in its teeth, which is why people say, "Don't look a gift horse in the mouth." The age-cups on a horse's teeth are worn smooth after about twelve years. That's where the term smooth-mouthed comes from. I've heard of horses living to be twenty-five or thirty years old, but those were mostly show horses or trick horses that had been exceptionally well cared for. A twenty-year-old horse that has worked on a farm all its life is a tired horse. Our sad old nags were all candidates for the fox farm.

"What does 'plug' mean?"

Aubrey looked down his nose at me. "A plug's an old horse that's all worked out, and not worth much anymore."

"Are all our horses plugs?"

He gave me another hard look. "I'd say Queen is still a pretty good horse, but the rest of them you could call plugs, no question about that."

That night, Queen stumbled into a dry ditch in the pasture, landed on her back and died there in the ditch. Aubrey found her the next morning when he went out to bring in the cows for milking.

If you were to pick the low point for Aubrey on the farm, I think that must have been it. He never talked about it, and I can only imagine how he felt. As a kid, I didn't give him credit for the courage it must have taken for him to carry on.

Queen had been one half of a team of bays. Lady was the other half, not a bad old horse, except that she was blind. We also had a bay coach horse called Bill, also blind. One evening Bill came plodding up to the barn with a dishpan stuck on a hind foot. He had stepped through it as it lay upside down in the pasture, and couldn't shake it off.

We worked Bill alongside Babe, a little black mare with a blaze face and white stockings. She was a good deal smaller than Bill, and they made an odd-looking team. Babe, one-eyed and so stiff in the knees she could hardly get her feet over the sill of the horse-barn door.

Last of the lot, and most pathetic of all, was our little black pony—the one I rode my first day on the farm. Maybe because she was black, someone named her Beauty. The poor old nag, she was a plug among plugs, blind and weak and slow, not up to doing anything much beyond carrying kids around on her back. Out of meanness or desperation, I never knew which it was, the old man put Beauty in harness, and took her out to work in the field. Half a day of it killed her.

They put a chain around her neck and dragged her back to the barn, her head bumping and dust all over her eyeballs. The old man haggled her open with an ax, and the hogs ate what was left of her. Her skull lay out in the orchard lot behind our house for a long time.

Beauty's skull was a reminder of the kinds of events on the farm over which we had little or no control. Livestock died from overwork, from old age, from any one of the countless diseases we seemed unable to prevent. I learned early on never to make a pet of a farm animal because it might die at any time.

All the rest of our horses were gone soon enough. Bill died in harness, hitched to the manure spreader. With no warning, he reared up and fell over backward, stone dead. Lady died from a little pebble, "a gravel," that worked its way into the quick of her left front hoof. Aubrey tied a poultice of millet seed on her foot, but the poor creature was beyond help. She agonized for days until even the old man took pity on her, and had her shot.

I don't know how he managed it, given our circumstances, but Aubrey replaced Queen and Lady with a nice team of middle-sized bays. We called the new pair by the same names as the old team. Like them, our new horses weren't exactly matched. Queen had a blaze face and white stockings, and was a bit taller than Lady, also a bay with a black mane and tail. Lady was a shade slower than Queen, but they worked well together, and they were a pleasure to drive.

Not long after we got the new bay team, Aubrey decided there might be money in raising draft horses. This in spite of the fact every farmer we knew was going into debt to buy a tractor. Aubrey bought a Belgian stallion with a fancy name, Byrnleigh. I thought his name was "Burnly," because that was the way it sounded to me. About the same time, Aubrey purchased a big sorrel brood mare we named Molly.

We kept the Belgian stallion at stud. He couldn't run loose in the pasture with the other stock, but had to live in a box stall in the barn "tied up by the head," as the law required.

Belgian draft horses are big animals. Byrnleigh stood about eighteen hands (six feet) high. A hand is four inches, with the measurement taken at the horse's shoulder, so Byrnleigh was fairly tall, but he was quiet and well behaved, never difficult to manage. Although strictly speaking it was illegal, we worked Byrnleigh teamed with Molly. They would go up alongside a noisy thrashing machine with no fuss or bother.

Some time after WW II, Aubrey got around to buying the farm

from his uncle, but before that, while Tom Willis still owned the place, he paid us visits now and then, quite properly to see how things were going. A Chinese proverb says the best fertilizer for any farm is the footprints of its landlord, and Uncle Tom seems to have thought so, too. He was an elegant-looking old gentleman when he was dressed up, but there was something fake about him, and he was the cause of my parents faking a little, too.

Mary Willis, Uncle Tom's wife, we believed was genuinely pious, and my uncle did a finished job of pretending to be. My parents ducked and weaved during our landlord's visits, especially where profanity was concerned. Aubrey swore like a sergeant-major, and Maude could unburden herself if the occasion called for it, but when Uncle Tom and Aunt Mary stayed with us, no one said so much as damn.

During those visits, we began every meal with my mother's invitation to Uncle Tom to ask the blessing, a thing we never did at any other time, believe me. With my uncle there, we all made a show of bowing our heads while he murmured his formula in what I suppose he took to be an appropriate tone.

I had been warned about what was expected of me, but when my younger brother came along nobody thought to brief him. On this occasion he was about three years old. Everyone at the table was in the required attitude of devotion, and Uncle Tom gathered his strength. The silence was broken when Morey piped up, "What us doing, Maude?"

It was during one of our landlord's visits that Byrnleigh raised a fuss, the only time he did anything of the sort. Uncle Tom had stepped into the barn beside Byrnleigh's stall, and, without any warning, reached out and slapped the horse on the rump. Startled, and I presume, affronted, Byrnleigh proceeded methodically to kick out the side of the barn behind him.

I happened to be coming out of the house at just that moment, and it looked like something out of a comic strip, pieces of barn flying all over the place. I took it as a lesson in common civility. Always speak to the horse before you put a hand on him. That's hardly too much to ask. I guess you might apply the same rule to people, to girls at least.

During the time we had Byrnleigh at stud, Aubrey asked a fee of fifteen dollars for "a standing colt." If the fee wasn't paid, the law said the owner of the stallion could take the colt in lieu of fee. Most paid. Some didn't, but Aubrey never claimed a colt for an unpaid stud fee.

Then came a disaster. Byrnleigh went blind. He had developed a condition called "wolf teeth." What would be eyeteeth in a human being grew abnormally long roots, pressing on the horse's optic nerve and robbing him of his sight. That put an end to his services at stud. Nobody wanted to pay for a colt sired by a blind horse.

A year or so later, Aubrey had Byrnleigh out in the field with Molly, plowing corn. It was a hot Sunday morning in July, not a day when he should have been in the field. Aubrey was prone to weird moves, but it was so hot that the old man came in from the field in the middle of the morning, watered the team, turned Molly out to pasture and put Byrnleigh in the barn. It was Sunday, and the Fourth of July, so Aubrey and I went to see the motor boat races on the Amana lily pond—a regular Fourth of July event. When we came home we found our beautiful Belgian horse dead in his stall.

Neck-Deep on a Tall Man

"What are the roads like where you're moving?" It was the first question people asked when they heard we were going to farm. The answer, "Dirt," brought sympathetic clucking noises and a change of subject.

Iowa with its ninety-nine counties was admitted to the Union in 1844, organized on principles established in the time of Andrew Jackson, with very little changed since then. When a county is laid out, the idea is that the county seat and its court house be so situated that a farmer could drive to town with his team, transact his business at the court house and drive home again, all in one day. It worked well enough for Andrew Jackson.

In Iowa, all county officials, except the Supervisors in charge of road maintenance, were chosen by ballot. Please note that the Supervisors were the only officials in the county who have authority to spend money, therefore they were the only ones with any real power, but in Iowa they were appointed, not elected. Nobody gave much thought to revising the system.

I loved to ride my pony along our dirt roads. There was no gravel to hurt her feet, and in spring wild plum blossoms smelled so sweet I almost fell out of the saddle, drunk on perfumed air.

Radio provided our entertainment at home, and the party-line telephone kept us in touch with neighbors and friends in town, but it was over dirt roads that we went to transact our day-to-day business. We drove to town to sell eggs and cream, and to buy groceries and ice. The Bricker brothers came around with their truck to pick up the bulk milk we sold to a creamery thirty miles away in Cedar Rapids.

I stood in the yard and looked west down that empty strip of clay ruts bobbling over low hills toward the sunset. Our yellow clay road was my path to the unknown, a link to my friends in town, to a better school and to places where there was less hard work. In my imagination it was a golden highway, but the road in my mind, I discovered later, ran only one way. Older people told me, "Oh, you'll want to come back here someday, no matter what you think now." I never believed it.

I learned how to drive on muddy roads by watching Aubrey. He looked as if he were wrestling with the wheel, fighting the car, trying to keep it moving and staying out of the ditch at the same time. It was exciting, but it was worrisome, too. When the going was tough, Aubrey tended to flare up at anyone near him.

With ruts so deep the bottom of the car dragged in the mud, you could actually take your hands off the steering wheel and let the car follow the track on its own, provided you didn't try to go too fast. I did that to show off the first time I brought a girl home from college. She was from Chicago, and while we went wallowing along through those hub-deep ruts, she told me she didn't think she wanted to live in the country.

The road east of our farm was a mile of dirt leading to a paved highway, Iowa 149, nicknamed the washboard because it was so hilly. If you went west from our place, there was a mile of dirt to a cross-road, then another mile north to US Highway 6. It was a shorter pull to the east, but the hills were steeper. Going west was twice as far, but it wasn't quite so hilly.

There was always an argument about which way to go when the roads were bad. Either way, we had to deal with some serious mud. We wrangled it over time after time, but I don't recall that anybody ever had a final word on the subject.

Late in the fall of 1935, we were in town one Saturday night when the rain began to come down in sheets. I knew our old Model-T wasn't up to getting us home through deep mud, and I was worried. I thought my mother seemed just a bit too unconcerned when she suggested we walk over to the Ford Garage, Simmons' Motor Company. There was a shiny new gray Ford V-8 waiting for us. I couldn't have been more surprised if I she had presented me with an airplane. Ford was bringing out its new cars for 1936, and the old man had made a good bargain on last year's model.

Our new Ford got a proper baptism. We were doing all right, sloshing and grinding our way home through the clay ruts, but when Aubrey tried to turn off the road into the garage, we slid down the grade into our middle yard, and couldn't get back on the road. The new car spent its first night at home standing out in the rain.

John Jacobi, one of our neighbors, was in charge of what little road maintenance we had. He was hired by the county to put the roads in order after a rain. John had a small road scraper pulled by a four-horse team, and after a rain when the road had begun to dry but was not yet rock-hard, he came past our house with his team and scraper filling the ruts with clods. The parallel ruts in our road looked like worm paths under the bark when you pull it off a dead tree trunk.

When the roads began to dry off after a rain you straddled the deep ruts as you drove. There were then two sets of tracks—one cut deep in the clay, and a second, smoother, relatively straight set of tracks that ran between the twisty ruts. For all practical purposes, it was a one-way road. Cautious drivers pulled to the right before going over the top of a hill, avoiding a head-on collision with anyone coming from the opposite direction. Daredevils just blasted along, depending on luck and their reflexes to protect them from disaster. Fern Timm was one of the fastest drivers in the neighborhood. I visited Fern in Iowa a couple of years ago. She was then over 90 years old. She offered to drive when we went out for lunch, but I talked her out of it.

In August and September when the corn was tall in the fields, every corner was a blind corner and a hazard, except that our dry clay roads had a built-in safety feature. Huge roils of dust rising behind any fast-moving car could be seen for miles, even though the car itself might be out of sight. Wagons pulled by horses or tractors didn't raise much dust, and anyone driving a tractor or a team knew he had to look sharp at blind corners.

After a rain, I kept an eye out for the road scraper. John Jacobi was a good old man who let me sit on the rear platform of the machine as he drove. John never needed to be asked. All I had to do was wave to him, and he pulled up and let me climb on board.

Most of the time a neighbor kid from down the road, Jimmie Hartz, would already have hitched a ride, and the two of us went along together, swinging our legs, over the hills to the highway and back. John drove his team with the lines knotted over his shoulder like a plowman, his hands free to work the vertical wheels controlling the angle and depth of the machine's scraper blade.

John liked to stop under the shade of a big oak tree in front of our house to let his team catch their breath while he talked with my dad. Getting out his sack of Bull Durham and his cigarette papers, he would set about rolling a smoke. He was a nervous man, and he spoke very rapidly. I watched fascinated one day while John stuck a freshly rolled cigarette in his lips, continuing to speak with an unlighted match in his hand. The cigarette bobbed up and down, tobacco leaking out the end where he had failed to twist it tightly enough. When John finally struck the match on his thumbnail, the cigarette paper was empty, and it went up in a whoosh like a magician's flash paper.

I wish I could say everything ended happily for John, but he was a victim of what is now called spousal abuse. His wife and son treated him so badly that he went completely out of his head. One night they found him wandering around in a field stark naked. Later, the word was that he had died of neglect. Everybody knew the truth, but nothing was ever done about it.

Along with their many inconveniences, our unimproved roads had some pleasant features. In summer, masses of wild roses and flowering plums grew on the high, grassy banks along the roads. There was pussy willow in spring, and bitter sweet in the fall.

During the terrible drought years, the grassy road banks were a kind of resource, too. Our pastures were burned to a crisp early in the spring of 1934, the white clover blossoms so dry they crunched like toast underfoot. I helped Aubrey herd our cows along the road that spring letting them eat the grass growing outside the fences. I didn't understand anything about poverty or drought. For me, herding cows along the fence was just another game.

Winter was a different story. Then our roads with their high, brushy banks presented a different kind of problem. Winter winds in Iowa blow out of the north and northwest. Our road ran east and west, and when it snowed and the wind blew hard, the road drifted full of snow between the banks that had looked so pretty the summer before. Wind scouring across the snow formed a crust strong enough that a man could walk right over a fence supported by the drifted snow. I cut snow blocks to build forts, and dug caves in the drifts that lasted for weeks, shrinking down to the size of mole runs as the snow melted.

One family in our neighborhood lived east of us, and there were three more families living along the road to the west. After a storm all of us came together to dig out. We boys thought it was great fun, but we could quit and go into the house to warm up at the open oven door on the kitchen range when we got too cold or tired. I'm not so certain the men were all that fond of the exercise, especially when they had to do it time after time throughout the winter.

Late in the 1930s, about the time we began to enjoy the benefits of the Rural Electrification Administration, the Iowa County Supervisors decided they could afford to grade our roads. Grading didn't do much to improve our roads (they were still slick, sticky clay,) but now there were deep ditches on both sides to fall into if you slid off the road. Grading ripped out all the shrubs and flowers, and they never grew back.

After our roads were graded, County maintenance crews could clear them with tractors and plows when we were snowed in during the winter. I peered out from my bedroom window late one night, watching as the caterpillar and plow came shouldering through the drifts, headlights flashing in the dark, releasing us from our snowy prison—and knocking down our mailbox to boot.

When people talked about bad roads, Mrs. Fry's funeral was the benchmark for judging all bad road conditions. That lady was a dear, sweet little thing, long a widow, mother of our neighbor, Bernice Hartz. Mrs. Fry was a tiny woman who always, it seemed to me, wore a clean, starched housedress with a floral pattern, over which she pinned a clean, starched apron with still another floral pattern. She lived out her life in town, but when she died early in the spring of the year, the family decided to have her body brought out to the Hartz farm for the wake.

Wakes in our neighborhood were somber affairs. I was surprised years later when I learned about Irish wakes that were wild parties. Our wakes certainly weren't parties. Two people sat up with the corpse all night each night from the time of death until the funeral. They say the practice was a carry-over from the period before embalming, when people were afraid of being buried alive.

Mrs. Fry's wake was held on the farm where her daughter lived. The roads were frozen when they brought her body out to the farm, but on the day before the funeral we had a warm spell. Our roads were worst after a general thaw in the spring when "the frost came out." Then, they used to say, the bottom fell out of the roads. It wasn't much of an exaggeration, either, and that was exactly the situation when we laid Mrs. Fry to rest. The roads that day were neck-deep on a tall man.

They used a tractor to drag the hearse out to the farm over roads that looked like World War One battlefields. Tractors in corn country usually had narrow-set row crop front wheels. Clay mud balled up behind those wheels, making it almost impossible to steer the tractor, churning the road into one long sinkhole. Somehow they got the hearse with Mrs. Fry's body back to the cemetery.

Aubrey wasn't the best driver in the world when it came to mud roads. This once, however, he had better luck—at least he did on the way into town—and we made it to the highway under our own power. The Shedenhelm family had better sense than anybody else in the neighborhood. They pulled their car out to the highway with a team of horses.

Coming home was something else altogether. The Shedenhelms got through with their team, but the rest of us ended mired in to the axles. The clutch on our car burned out, leaving it helpless.

Everett Timm lived at the top of the hill that defeated us all. Everett was a big man with perfect teeth and a big smile who went about his work with a laugh and a joke. He got out his tractor and a wagon, loaded all the women and kids into it, and promised to deliver us home safely.

Everett must have been joking this time, too, because he didn't notice that the drawbar on his tractor was offset to the right when he hitched the wagon to it. As we moved out, Everett was laughing and talking with Aubrey, riding on the fender of the tractor, neither of them paying any attention to the wagon behind them as it edged its way toward the ditch. The mud was soft, and no one was hurt when the wagon ran off the road, and spilled us all out, but I have to say the women in that wagon were pretty peeved with Everett.

Dear sweet Mrs. Fry who never made a speck of trouble during her life was the cause of a major problem at the end of it. After that whenever anybody talked about bad roads, someone was sure to say, "You should have been here the day of Mrs. Fry's funeral."

February 1991

The drive to Marengo from the Iowa City/Cedar Rapids airport brought back a host of memories of life on the farm. Cedar Rapids was then the big city with streetcars and dime stores, the place where we went shopping, on those occasions when we had some extra money. Along the way was the Amana Freezer plant where my grandpa and I worked after I got home from the Army; a bakery and butcher shop in South Amana where Pop took me to do a little free-loading; and the farmhouses where my friends from country school once lived, places now looking run-down and shabby.

The Iowa State Highway markers that identified fatal accidents, including Miss Nelson, my first teacher in country school, were gone. Maybe in the end there had been too many of them. The bridge over Hilton Creek where twice I nearly got my everlastings—once when I fell down on the icy road and just missed being run over by a car, and again when I was almost shoved off a twenty-foot drop by a boy I was tussling with—was mainly unchanged. Over south, back of the hills, I could see the roof of the farmhouse where I grew up.

Two evergreens were all that remained on the site of my old school. I swerved to avoid the carcass of a deer lying half off the road on the shoulder. Number 6 was as narrow and dangerous as it had always been.

Aubrey holding Babe

"I Love Those Cows and Chickens (But This Is the Life!)"—*Comic Song*

In 1933, we kept twenty-four cows that we milked by hand. Aubrey was up and out bringing them from the pasture at four in the morning in the summertime. For some reason I didn't understand—and didn't inquire into, you can bet—they didn't make me get out of bed to do chores at that time of day. I was always a scrawny kid, and it may be my mother laid down the law that I needed my sleep. As a natural lay-about, I took it all in stride. It didn't occur to me to be ashamed of myself.

Aubrey liked to get up early. His temper was unpredictable, but he was almost always in a good mood in the morning. Maybe that's why I wasn't rousted out at dawn. The chores I had to do were all in the evening. My wife tells me I was spoiled. I guess she's right about that.

I was five years old when we moved to the farm, too small to help, so Aubrey, who didn't like to work alone, always tried to hire a man, someone who was willing to work by the month for his room and board and an unbelievably small salary. We had a string of these fellows, so many, in fact, that it got to be a neighborhood joke. Times were hard, but the men Aubrey hired wouldn't put up with his abuse.

Farm chores have to be done morning and night, day in and day out, come Hell, high water, or an old lady with a cane. Milking, feeding and watering livestock can't be postponed or skipped.

We were doing what was called "mixed farming" in the early 1930s, a variety of animals and a variety of crops, all of it on a very small scale. We had a few of everything on our farm: cattle, horses, hogs, sheep, and chickens. Daily chores were a matter of milking the cows, and of getting food and water to the rest of the stock. The work was heavier in the winter, when all the feed had to be laid out in troughs and mangers, and the stock tanks and watering troughs had to be cleared of ice. In summer our stock was turned out to pasture, requiring very little care beyond that.

Horses live in their stalls in the winter. When the weather was tolerable, we turned them out in the yards for a few hours every day to get some exercise, and to drink at the tank. Morning and evening we filled their mangers with fodder from the haymow. We fed our horses ear-corn that we carried from the crib to the barn in a metal silage basket holding a bushel and a half. When I could pick up a silage basket full of corn, set it up on my shoulder and carry it across the barnyard, I felt pretty grown up.

We fed our milk cows at their stanchions: hay along with some supplement like tankage, a stinking ground feed made from the carcasses of dead animals. All our cattle, including those we were fattening for market, got silage (chopped corn stalks fermented in a silo) with their fodder during the winter.

Silage had to be dug out of the silo, thrown down a chute, and then shoved around with a fork filling the feed trough. It was fed sparingly to the cows we milked. Too much of it gave a sour flavor to the milk. Something similar happens when milk cows are turned out on grass for the first time in the spring of the year. Then, for a week or so until their digestive systems got accustomed to the fresh pasture, our cows' milk had a strong grassy taste.

In freezing weather, all watering troughs had to be cleared of ice at least twice a day. I used a tool called a mattock, a combination of an ax and an adze, to chop ice out of the troughs. The adze end of the mattock tended to throw splinters of ice, mud and manure back in my face when I cleared the troughs. Using it gave me a much needed lesson in keeping my mouth shut.

Clearing ice from the stock tank outside the barn was a never-ending task in cold weather: building a fire in the tank heater, chopping away ice and getting it out of the tank. The float device that controlled the flow of water into the tank from the windmill regularly got out of whack and needed repair, always in freezing weather it seemed. Putting it right involved taking off your jacket, rolling up your sleeves and plunging into the icy water to get at the broken part.

The worst part of doing chores was working with hickory-handled pitchforks. Gripping one of those fork handles in cold weather was like clutching an icicle. My hands seemed to freeze to the fork. If I showed any discomfort, Aubrey was sure to notice, and then would come the sneering order I dreaded, "God damn it, go to the house if you're cold!"

Chores varied a little according to the kind of fodder we were feeding. For a year or so we fed soybean hay, not a particularly efficient forage, and certainly not pleasant stuff to handle. Cattle won't eat dry soybean stalks, and the residual clutter had to be cleared out of the mangers morning and night. Soybean hay also made clouds of black dust when it was handled—the leaves along with the food value they might contain falling off and breaking up—dust that coated the inside of my nose and throat. My handkerchiefs were stiff with clots of black snot.

My first regular chore at the barn—I was about six years old—was to stir warm, fresh milk in the ten-gallon cans that were to be sent off to market the next day. The cans of milk were set in the cool water of our stock tank outside the cow barn. Using a long metal paddle, I stirred the milk until Aubrey told me to stop. Cooling the fresh milk made it less likely to go sour before it was delivered to a creamery thirty miles away in Cedar Rapids.

Bringing in the cows for milking in the late afternoon was my next regular chore.

It was a natural. I could do it on my way home from school. If the cattle were being fed at their stanchions in the barn, they knew what to expect. When I got them up on their feet and headed for the barn, they would go the rest of the way on their own. I learned the hard way that when they were not being fed at the barn, they would just lie down again, leaving me to wonder what had become of them when I arrived home by a shorter route.

Bringing in even the sleepiest old milk cow is more of a problem when she has a new calf. The cow won't leave her calf, and the calf doesn't have sense enough to follow the cow. The only way you can make any progress at all is to nudge the calf along, letting the cow follow, except that it isn't quite so simple. Getting a new calf up on its feet, on its pins, as we used to say, is like setting up a collapsing toy.

I had seen pictures of cowboys carrying calves across the saddle or on their shoulders, but I wasn't riding a horse, and I was too small to hoist a calf onto my shoulders. I'm not sure the cow would have put up with that anyway. I had to urge the calf along, keeping a wary eye on the anxious cow, making sure she didn't butt me into the next county.

Raising chickens was the responsibility of a farm wife. It was light work, and kids helped their mothers with it. Before World War II, the money a farmer's wife made from her chickens was what she used to buy the food for her family, to "set the table." My mother made some special deal, I don't know the details, or how she managed it, with Uncle Tom, so that, even though we were farming "on shares," she did not have to divide her earnings from the sale of chickens and eggs with him.

After the war, inflation drove up the prices of commercial feed, while the selling price of eggs was held down by price controls. Then the profit went out of raising chickens on small farms, but in the 1930s we raised our little flock from day-old chicks we bought a hundred or so at a time.

The Iowa County Hatchery charged $7.75 for a hundred chicks. If you bought 500 or more, the price was $7.25 a hundred, and if you were able to pay cash in advance, you got an even better price—$6.75 a hundred. They arrived in crates squared off into quarters, each section holding a dozen or so of the downy, peep-peeping little things, with a tin cup half full of water wired securely into each corner of the crate. Day-old chicks were so small I could hold two or three of them in one hand. They looked like live Easter toys, but they soon grew out of that attractive stage.

We had several breeds of chickens to choose from. Rhode Island Reds were especially flashy looking, the roosters with beautiful iridescent tail feathers. Leghorns were white chickens reputed to be good egg-producers, although the eggs they laid were small. Plymouth Rocks had gray feathers, were somewhat heavier than Leghorns and laid larger eggs. Plymouth Rock eggs had brownish-tan shells, while Leghorn eggs were snow white.

Some people imagine they can taste a difference between white eggs and brown eggs, but that is old wives' nonsense. The food chickens eat, not the color of eggshells, is what determines the flavor of eggs. Chickens fed on fish waste, for example, will produce fishy-tasting eggs. During the hot, dry summers of 1934 and '35 we endured plagues of grasshoppers. Our chickens gorged themselves on the pests, and we thought that was a good thing—until the eggs began to taste a little off.

The floor of the chicken coop had to be kept covered with litter so that the chicks could not peck at their own droppings. Maude experimented endlessly with various kinds of bedding: wood shavings, shredded newspaper and God knows what else. You might think straw is an obvious choice, but straw bedding is too coarse for baby chicks. They get lost in it.

Chicks not only peck at their droppings, they also peck at each other. There were patent medicines that claimed they prevented cannibalism, but nothing really worked. You can rely on it; the odd-colored chick will be pecked to death. Collegiality has about as much play among chickens as it has among academics.

Oats and corn were too coarse to be fed to chickens until they were at least six weeks old, and then the grain had to be thoroughly processed in a feed grinder. When we could afford it, we bought commercial feed in hundred-pound sacks from stores in town.

For years, hard-pressed farm wives had made feed sacks into dishtowels, rough aprons and whatnot. The manufacturers caught on, and began to print feed sacks in floral patterns. That's a pretty blunt marketing ploy, but it worked. Farm wives used printed sacking for dresses, aprons, pot holders, sun bonnets—almost any article of clothing you would care to name, and some better left nameless. Squeezed by hard times, they did the best they could with what they had.

Having eaten all their dry food, chickens drank a great deal of water. We didn't have running water on our farm. Every drop had to be carried to the chickens in buckets. We used all combinations of patented devices for watering chicks: tanks, float-valves and water trays, each one claiming to be the most convenient and efficient.

Chickens walk in anything and everything, and they quickly slime their watering pans with the gunk they pick up on their feet. It is best to clean the mess away at each watering before it builds up and becomes really obnoxious.

Winter adds to the watering problem. Livestock have to drink whether or not the temperature is below freezing. We didn't have electricity on the farm until late in the '30s, so our watering fountains were equipped with kerosene burners to keep them free of ice. Those lamps had to be filled daily, the wicks trimmed, and the heated fountains placed so as to reduce fire hazard. Later, the fountains heated with electricity were safer, but still it was a task to be done every day, twice a day.

Cleaning chicken coops is a particularly nasty job. Chicken manure breaks up into an acrid dust, building up in layers on the floor of the coops. You can't get a shovel into the stuff, and it falls apart when you try to use a manure fork. Among the many really dirty jobs the farm has to offer, cleaning the chicken house ranks pretty well up toward the top on the disagreeable scale. Maude and I cleaned the chicken coops. Aubrey made his contribution by leaving an empty manure spreader close by for our convenience.

Like infants of any kind, little chickens have to be tended at every turn. In the cool evenings, they must be shooed into their coops, and the doors made fast against predators. The lot north of the house where we kept our baby chicks grew thick with dog fennel, and a whiff of crushed fennel still reminds me of getting the chickens shut up for the night.

One Saturday night we went off to town, but forgot to secure our chickens properly. When we came home, a possum had got in with them, and had killed a dozen or so. My mother screamed and cried and made a great pow-wow when she saw what had happened.

Possums are ugly little critters with a bogus loveable-ness in the public mind because of the comic strip, *Pogo*. In real life they are nocturnal killers, omnivores, slow moving, and rather stupid, with a double row of pointed teeth that makes them thoroughly unpleasant adversaries.

When the raider wasn't a possum, it might have been a red fox or a raccoon, both agile killer-thieves. I've also seen hawks swoop down and fly away with chicks in their talons. Old-time farmers kept a few guinea hens among their chickens, heavy birds with slate-gray feathers speckled in white, and heads that seem too small for their bodies. Hawks are supposed to be afraid of guineas, but I can't vouch for the truth of that.

Bull snakes, harmless but scary, curled themselves up in chicken's nests to feed on the eggs laid there. Snakes swallow whatever they eat whole and digest it later. You could see how many eggs the snake had taken by counting the lumps in its body.

One of our hired men showed me how to kill a snake, taking it by the tip of the tail and snapping its head the way you would a whip. I could never bring myself to get a firm grip on the tail of a snake. They aren't slimy, but the skin is cold, and you can feel the muscles working under it. Bull snakes eat mice as well as eggs, making for some kind of ecological balance, I suppose, but when we found a snake in the henhouse, the snake was the loser.

Roosters in the flock were culled out and sold to keep them from fertilizing the eggs and reducing their value. A fertile egg shows a tiny blood spot on the yoke when it is opened. People who bought eggs objected to the decoration, and the price went down accordingly. With or without roosters, however, hens get "broody." Following her instincts, a hen will build a nest hidden away, lay a dozen or more eggs in it, and then sit on them to hatch them out. Eggs that haven't had the benefit of a rooster don't hatch; they just spoil.

Young chickens are called pullets, and pullet eggs are small, so small that the produce buyers wouldn't accept them. We used the small eggs for cooking. Some hens laid eggs with double yolks. Extra-large eggs weren't accepted at the market; we kept them for our own use.

When hens start laying, they need a dietary supplement called oyster shell, which is exactly what the name says it is, the shells of oysters or clams ground into flakes. We bought oyster shell from the Marengo Grain Company, a hundred pounds for ninety cents. When hens eat the stuff, they produce eggs with hard, firm shells. Without oyster shell, the hens lay eggs with soft, leathery outsides. You can't crack an egg like that. They have to be opened with a pair of sharp-pointed scissors. You can't sell leather-skinned eggs, either.

Gathering eggs was one of my chores. I was carrying a small tub full of eggs, when I had the bad luck to stumble and broke some of them. Aubrey saw what happened.

"What the hell are you doing? Pick up your goddamned feet."

"I'm sorry."

"Yeah, well 'I'm sorry' doesn't buy any groceries."

I was usually the one who discovered nests that were hidden away. The first thing I had to do then was to see if the eggs were fit to eat, testing them by putting them in a tub of water. If they floated or stood on end they were too stale to be used.

It was no use trying to cheat by spreading the suspect eggs around in a case full of fresh ones, hoping they wouldn't be noticed. Eggs were "candled" by the buyers in town—held up, two at a time, in front of a strong light source to check their quality. Spoiled eggs showed a dark yolk. They were tossed out, and the price on the rest of the crate was docked. Very often all the eggs in one of the nests I found had gone bad. Then I had the fun of pitching them at a telephone pole across the road.

We took eggs to market in town once a week, carrying them in a small, cube-shaped twelve-dozen crate, or, later, in a double crate that held twenty-four dozen. Dimpled cardboard dividers held eggs standing on end, with folding cardboard pieces that opened up and were set between the eggs to keep them from bumping together and breaking. I thought we were really moving ahead when our hens produced so many eggs that we had to use a double crate to hold them.

In 1933, eggs brought eleven cents a dozen, and that price didn't improve for years. By 1940, eggs were up three cents on average, to fourteen cents a dozen. After the war, in 1946, the price went as high as thirty-three cents. I'm glad I never had to explain it to the hens.

While the term "chicken farming" was synonymous in those days with anything done on a small scale, there was still something very satisfying about gathering a bucketful of eggs. Eggs were treasure, and gathering them was pure fun. We used to laugh about Aubrey's going out to gather the eggs about twenty times a day when a new flock of chickens began to produce.

Barnyards are covered with the manure of livestock penned there. When it rained, the condition of our barnyard was made worse by a little ditch that drained a field across the road from us. In the spring, or after a rain, the ditch turned our barnyard into a swamp, and we plunged in up to our butts in stinking ooze.

In the middle of the quagmire was what we euphemistically called "the milk house," a building set on a concrete slab rising like an island out of a sea of muck. Under the milk house was a shallow well, a so-called dug well, a pit about twenty-five feet deep and three or four feet across, lined with brick, and covered with a steel plate on which a pump was mounted. Up the slope from the well was a concrete feeding platform, and a small hog house. In other words, we had an open well set directly in the flow of animal wastes. Nobody gave it a thought.

Water from that well was icy cold, and it had a good flavor—as well it might have had—and we all, neighbors included, drank it with relish, until one day we found the pump clogged with fur and body parts of drowned rats, at which point we give up our good-tasting water. God alone knows why we didn't all die of typhoid, but nobody got so much as a stomachache from it. When my parents sold out in the 1970s, the people who bought the farm wisely tore the milk house down and filled in the well. Today it exists only as a memory, where it can't do much harm.

The milk house was rotten dirty, stinking of sour milk. Now and then Aubrey ordered me to clean it. I hated anything that required making an effort, especially in a lost cause, but with no choice in the matter, I reluctantly got a shovel and a broom, and set about scraping and brushing the walls and floor to get rid of the worst of the filth. The place was never sprayed with anything to disinfect it, nor was it ever whitewashed. My efforts got rid of the worst of the rat droppings, the cobwebs, and the dead granddaddy-long-legs, but that's about the best you could say for it. A granddaddy-long-legs is an interesting bug, by the way. He carries a deadly poison, but he's harmless because he can't bite.

From the time I was old enough to be aware of comparisons, I wanted to be big-boned and muscular like the other farm boys in our neighborhood. To make up for my spindly build, I flew into my work the way I saw Aubrey do. I heard some fast-moving fellow described, "By God, he's a hustler." I wanted people to say that about me, and I pitched into my work like crazy. The result of all that fakery was my coming to loath physical exertion of any kind, in spite of which I never lost the habit of driving headlong at any task assigned me.

From 1933 until about 1938, we milked our twenty-four cows by hand. For the benefit of those who have never been on a farm, milking has to be done morning and evening, and on a strict schedule. Varying milking time by as little as fifteen minutes can cause a significant drop in milk production. Think about that, and put an end to any ideas you may have about the freedom and independence of farmers.

Independence, I believe, is a myth perpetuated by farmers to make up for the fact they have to work so hard for next to nothing. Far from being free, farmers are slaves to their land, indentured to their livestock and the weather, not to mention market forces beyond their control.

The equipment we needed for milking was simple: buckets, milking stools, a big metal strainer and ten-gallon cans to hold bulk milk. Today you can find ten-gallon milk cans for sale in any antique store, reflecting what I take to be a high incidence of brain softening in the population.

Our milk stools were homemade affairs fashioned out of pieces of 2 x 4. Two sticks a foot long were nailed together to form the leg of the stool, and another bit, about eight inches long, was tacked across the end to serve as a seat. They looked precarious, but it wasn't much of a trick to balance on one of them.

I learned to milk when I was about eight years old, and from then on, as long as we had dairy cows, I milked a cow or two as part of my chores. When I first started to milk, I was too small to hold the bucket between my knees, and had to set it flat on the floor instead. I thought I was pretty big when I could hold the bucket in the proper way, raising a thick layer of foam as I milked. I learned to milk "wet," squirting some milk on your hands makes them slip readily on the cow's teats. You can milk much faster that way, but it is obviously unsanitary.

My hands were usually clean, however I can assure you the cows' udders and teats were not. When the cows came in plastered with mud and manure, we scraped off the worst of it with our bare hands, and milked away. Olive-brown droplets fell into the buckets, disappearing into the thick layer of foam a fast milker raises in his pail. We strained this slurry through discs of cotton and gauze we bought at the hardware store in town. Our barnyard cats loved the milk-soaked strainer gauzes, gulping them down with relish.

Aubrey had graduated from the agricultural school of Iowa State University at Ames, and he knew better than to tolerate such conditions, but we never did a thing to clean up our cows before milking. I was in no position to be an innovator, even if I had been so inclined, which I wasn't.

Before DDT and the other insect killers that came out of World

War II, we had flies by the wagonload. Workers and cows alike were tormented by swarms of them in warm weather. You find yourself getting pretty familiar with the cow when you milk by hand, snuggling up close to her and burying your head in her flank so that she can't get a clear kick at you should the spirit so move her.

Too hard-up to buy commercial fly spray, we improvised our own, half kerosene and half lubricating oil, and sprayed it on the cattle. It worked fairly well. Still, I remember the sting of a cow's tail wrapping itself around my head and cutting me across the eyes as I milked. And when that tail was saturated with manure, well, so much the more memorable.

It was fine, too, in winter when the cows came in coated with ice from a sleet storm. Then as the ice melted and fell away from the cow's hide, it found its way down my neck while I worked. Then there were times when some poor animal got tangled in a badly maintained fence, and came to the barn with her teats slashed by barbed wire. I rubbed a patent medicine called Bag Balm, still on the market, by the way, into the cuts to ease her suffering. It seemed to help a little, softening the tissue and promoting healing, but a cow badly cut up often would not stand the pain, and had to be hobbled before she could be milked.

Hobbles were broad, hook-like flat metal pieces on a chain. They fit over the hocks on each hind leg, and were then pulled up tight. Cows didn't take kindly to any part of that sort of business. Having learned to recognize the jingling hobbles when they were about to be restrained, they went hopping around and kicking, making hobbling them a pretty dicey business. Taking a set of hobbles off after milking could be as much of an adventure as putting them on had been.

Learning to avoid a kick from the cow you are milking takes no more than extraordinary sensitivity and the reaction time of a chipmunk. I had more than one cow's hoof in my bucket before I learned to recognize the signals. Aubrey raised particular hell with me if I spilled any milk, and I polished the responses I needed in order to snatch my bucket away in one hand, my milk stool in the other, and then jump back to safety.

Avoiding a kick from the cow standing behind me was another matter. That blow across the small of my back seemed to come out of nowhere, and for no reason. I never quite figured it out. What had I done that made her want to kick me in the first place?

Maude took the milk we brought her for the kitchen, and strained it a second time using a kitchen sieve and a piece of clean cloth. Beyond that, we put all questions of sanitation out of our minds. By rights, we should all have died of undulant fever, but, as with the good-tasting water from our barnyard well, some higher power seems to have been on the lookout, keeping us alive and healthy. Then again, it may have been part of that peck of dirt my grandma said we were fated to eat before we died. I knew farm kids who drank raw milk and liked it, but from the time I saw where the stuff came from, I dropped it from my diet.

Farm prices during the '30s were desperately low. Corn was twenty-seven cents a bushel; oats were twenty cents a bushel. In Chicago, hogs went for from three to four cents a pound. There was a World's Fair in Chicago from 1933 to 1934, and Aubrey said, "If hogs go to six cents, we'll go to the World's Fair." It was a sorry kind of joke. Hogs were never going to bring that much money. He might as well have said we'll go to the fair if a sow flies over the barn.

We sold whole milk to a creamery in Cedar Rapids, about thirty miles away from our farm. The price in 1930 was a little over two cents a pound, two dollars a hundredweight. By 1933 it had fallen to just over a penny a pound, and it didn't rise to two cents again until 1942.

The bulk milk we sent to Cedar Rapids was picked up on a truck driven by the Bricker brothers, Harv and Marv. Muscular from head to foot, both of them, they got their dual-wheeled truck through to us no matter how bad the roads were.

Milk weighs about eight pounds a gallon. At a penny a pound, a ten-gallon can of milk brought us eighty cents, a princely return on all the drudgery required to get it. Depending on the season of the year, the number of cows we were milking and their yield, we sent from thirty to forty gallons of milk to market every day.

That earned us roughly eighty-four dollars a month. That was our milk check, the money we had to live on, but we were farming on shares, remember, and half of what we got for milk went to Uncle Tom. Out of the remaining forty-two dollars, Aubrey paid a hired man twenty-five dollars a month, and Maude fed him. And we had to pay the Bricker brothers for transporting our milk to market. You can begin to see we were cutting pretty close to the bone. I was too young to understand how tight our situation was. Looking back, I don't know how my parents did it.

What did we pay for the things we had to buy in the '30s? A carton of 200 Lucky Strike cigarettes cost $1.51. The cigarettes you bought in stores were called "tailor-made," but most men on the farm rolled their own. A bag of Bull Durham tobacco and the cigarette papers to go with it cost a nickel. Seasoned freeloaders bummed tailor-made cigarettes, and repaid with Bull Durham and papers.

Gode's Dry Goods sold women's spring frocks for from $3.95 to $5.95, and spring coats for $6.75 to $15. A five-month subscription to the *Atlantic Monthly* cost one dollar, although I confess I didn't know anybody who read the *Atlantic* .

The Trading Post ran an ad in our weekly paper, the Pioneer Republican, explaining their "cash to all" policy: "Credit to all," they said, would mean 10 to 20% higher prices, which says something about how far merchants felt they could trust their customers.

Remember, too, our milk checks were a gross return, taking nothing into account for the cost of production. Most farmers had only the most primitive methods for sorting out their income, if they used any at all. Cost accounting was an alien concept, a foreign language. If a farmer had a bank account, and in those days most did not, he was likely to rely on his checkbook balance to tell him how he was doing, and therefore had no real notion of whether he was making money or starving to death. More than one farmer woke one day to find he was dead broke, without the slightest idea of how he got that way. Gradually some farmers came to see that small-scale dairy operations were less than a break-even proposition. In our neighborhood all but one family had dropped out of dairying by the start of the Second War.

After we stopped selling whole milk and kept only eight or ten cows, we separated the milk we produced, and sold the cream in Marengo at the same place we sold our eggs. That was our source of ready money, however small.

Our separator, a hand-turned machine, was set up in the milk house. Aubrey and I lugged ten-gallon cans of milk from the cow barn across the bog of our barnyard to that abominable little shed. A crank on one side of the separator turned it. There was a tiny hammer hinged on the crank that tapped twice with each turn of the handle. As the machine was turned faster, centrifugal force held the hammer in place, and the tapping stopped. If you were working alone, it was a good trick to maintain separator speed while replenishing the supply of whole milk in the bowl.

A key on the big bowl at the top of the machine was opened, and milk began to run through. Cream, lighter in weight, came out of an upper spout in a thin stream, and skim milk emerged in a much larger stream from a lower spout. We soaked whole oats in the skim milk, and fed that slop to our hogs.

One milking from our few cows was never enough to fill our three-gallon container with cream. The cream we did get, we carried up to the house, and stored in the basement to keep it reasonably cool until we had a full container to sell in town.

Two or three places in Marengo bought eggs and cream from farmers. The principal one, Swift's, was part of the packinghouse chain buying chickens, eggs and cream for market in Chicago. There were also one or two grocery stores that bought eggs and cream, hoping farm wives would shop for their groceries in the same store. We never doubted the produce buyers were crooked, and we took our meager goods to market with a wary eye out for cheats. One of these characters, a fellow named Hank Johnson, somewhat the worse for booze at the time, had been heard to say, "There's more than one way to skin a farmer!" We dealt with old Hank because we had to, but we kept an eye on him.

In all but the bitterest winter weather, my mother washed the milking and separating equipment out in back of the house, dragging out scalding water from the kitchen, and adding Sal Soda to it. The gear was air-dried on a bench out in the open. In the winter, she hauled all the milking stuff down to the basement for washing.

In spite of her aversion to filth, not to mention that she had more than enough of her own to do at the house, Maude sometimes helped out with the milking, especially during those times when we had no hired man. It was never a good fit, bringing my mother's obsession with cleanliness headlong into the filth Aubrey tolerated at the barn.

Maude's participation ended abruptly one night when a cow, for no apparent reason, kicked her from one side of the walkway to the other as she was carrying a bucket of milk. She had a sharp imprint of a hoof on her hip for quite a while after the event. She never went back, but she told the story for a long time.

That's what it was like, day in and day out, on the farm. Town was a different kind of place. That's where I wanted to be.

Aubrey with Birnleigh (*c.*) and Molly

Plow and Plant

When families move today, they do it in the fall of the year in order to be settled in their homes in time for the kids to start to school, but our rural society in the 1930s was still dominated by the laws of the seasons and the ancient rhythms of agriculture: plow, plant and harvest. Moving day back then was the first of March, so that farmers could be on their land in time to get their crops in the ground.

Black soil on the Iowa river-bottom lands was as much as six feet deep in places. Aubrey told me he knew of fields that had been planted in corn every year since the prairie soil was first broken in the 19th century. We lived on an upland farm, away from the rich river bottoms, which meant we had to rotate our crops. In the clay hills we worked, a field might typically be in corn one year, small grain (oats or wheat) the next, and hay or soybeans the year following.

Grass seed was expensive. In 1933, alfalfa seed cost $19.50 a hundred weight, red clover was $15 and white clover $7.20.

In the Midwest, the principal crop, corn, was planted next. An old-time jingle warned:

The lazy farmer rues the day
He plants his corn past the 10th of May.

Another bit of folk wisdom had it that corn should be planted when oak leaves were the size of a squirrel's ear. Before any planting could be done, however, the fields had to be made ready. When the soil was dry enough that the plows would "scour clean," farmers hitched up their teams or got out their tractors and started to work.

When we moved to the farm, I suppose no more than half the people around us worked with tractors. In school, we boys thought we were shrewd forecasters when we said that pretty soon you would have to go to a circus to see a horse. Today, when most of the draft animals on farms—if you can find them at all—are show teams, what we thought were wild guesses have come true. By the end of WW II, almost nobody used horses, and today you have to go to an Amish farm to see a six-horse team on a gangplow or a harrow.

We thought our gangplows were big with their two plowshares turning the soil over in furrows as much as a foot deep. We didn't foresee the enormous tractor rigs with eight or ten plowshares that came along twenty years later. When that kind of equipment was used to get ready for planting, it was called deep plowing. What was really deep about it was the debt farmers went into in order to buy machinery like that.

Every farm used to have an old-fashioned walking plow. The implement gets its name from the fact the driver walked behind his team and plow. Today, you see walking plows set up as mounts for mailboxes. Years ago, farmers used walking plows to prepare their garden plots, but nobody used them to do any serious work in the field. As a kid, I actually plowed a round or two with a walking plow— with Aubrey one step behind me keeping an eagle eye on what I was doing.

Working with a walking plow looks easy, but it might be well to look again. However steady the team may be, they walk too fast for a beginner. It is easy to wobble off the path and begin plowing more or less at random—earning some caustic comments from the old man. If I pulled up in the plow handles, the plow dived deeper into the earth, while pushing down on the handles made it pop out of the ground like a squeezed watermelon seed. Aubrey's idea of a joke was to say using a walking plow was just like riding a bicycle except that you didn't have to pedal. It is true, you steered the thing by leaning it in the direction you wanted it to go, just as you do on a bike. You need both hands to hold the plow, and so a plowman ties the ends of the lines together, and loops them over his shoulder, over one arm and under the other. He controls his team with his voice, and with an occasional tug on the lines.

I read somewhere that an expert plowman with a good team could plow as much as four acres in a day with a walking plow, but I think he would have had to work from the crack of dawn until after dark to do it.

Poverty exposed farmers to some awful dangers. A family named

Eichhorn lived on the farm east of us, trying to make a living on eighty acres of clay hills. The wife was working alone in the field one day, preparing a patch of ground for planting, with one section of harrow hitched behind her two-horse team. The lines on the old harness she was using were too short, and she was walking in front of the harrow, directly behind the horses. She must have caught her heel under the harrow, because she fell with the harrow on top of her. Fortunately for her, she was driving an old, broken-down team, and when she yelled, "Whoa!" they stopped gratefully. A neighbor passing by on the road heard her screaming, and found her lying on her back, holding the harrow off her body in both hands. His chance passing and a team so old and decrepit they could barely walk saved her from horrible mutilation or death.

Once the field was harrowed smooth, it was ready for planting. Today, corn is planted with tractor-pulled machines that plant sixteen rows at a time, machines so large they have to be folded back on themselves to get through a gate. Before the war, corn was planted with little two-row outfits pulled by two horses.

Henry Wallace, Franklin Roosevelt's vice president during his third term, made a real contribution to the well being of farmers with his Pioneer Hybrid Seed Corn Company. Prior to the innovation of specially engineered seed corn, getting enough grain together for planting was a long, complicated process. When I was a boy, farmers were still selecting seed corn the old-fashioned way, using what they called a "rag doll tester."

The first step was to pick out some likely looking ears from last year's harvest, ears that showed good qualities in length, girth and depth of kernel. Selected ears were laid out on the floor in numbered spaces. A few kernels were taken from the ends of each ear, and from the middle. They were placed in numbered squares on a large piece of cotton flannel, the number of the square matching the number on the floor for the ear from which the kernels were taken.

Next, the flannel was rolled up very carefully so as not to disturb the grain, and one end of the roll—the rag doll—was laid flat in a shallow pan of water. Osmosis drew water up the flannel moistening the entire roll, and after a few days, the roll was gently opened and the kernels were checked to see which of them had sprouted.

Ears from which sprouted kernels had come were reserved for seed; the others were tossed back into the crib and the whole process was repeated until there was enough seed for planting.

My friend Carroll Gunderson tells me it took about a bushel of shelled corn to plant five acres back when corn was planted in "hills." A family farm of 200 acres with forty acres in corn would need at least eight bushels of shelled corn.

It was possible, even before the advent of Henry Wallace's Seed Corn Company, to buy seed in town, but the price was high, $4 a bushel in 1936. Remember that a farm hand earned his room and board plus a dollar a day, and you can see why most farmers went through the extra work to select their own seed corn rather than pay town prices—four days' wages for a bushel of seed.

When it has been planted properly, a newly sprouted field of corn shows up in the prettiest pattern. You can sight along the rows the length and breadth of the field, or you can "row" them obliquely from one corner of the field to the other. Farmers took as much pride in a well-planted field as their wives did in a neatly made quilt.

Some farmers had a flair for planting corn; some didn't. Farmers liked to needle each other about cornrows that had been warped by the sunshine. Uncle Tom, blind in one eye as the result of a boyhood accident, always claimed he could plant corn straight as a rifle shot because he had only one eye, but you are under no obligation to believe that.

If all went well, if we got the rain we needed, and if the summer nights were hot—"so hot you can hear the corn grow," corn planted early in May would be "knee-high by the Fourth of July." Today's fast-growing corn can be as tall as a man early in July, but, during the times I am talking about, the corn would probably have come up to a man's knees, and it would have been cultivated—the weeds plowed out of it—for the third time, after which it was "laid by." That meant the corn was on its own for the rest of the season.

Plowing corn with a two-wheeled horse-drawn plow was a tedious job. Those little machines took one row at a time, and seemed to crawl through the fields with the men plowing intent on their work, careful to take out the weeds and leave the corn. Here again, a quiet, steady team of horses was a major factor—if you didn't want to lose your mind.

The driver tied the reins around his back, looping them over one shoulder and under his other arm, because he needed both hands, and both feet, to guide the cultivator. Generally it went well enough, even if at an excruciatingly slow pace, except for those times when the flies were bad, and the horses fought them with their heads, tails and feet. My grandma always said flies bite harder just before a rain, another bit of her weather-forecasting lore that turned out to be true.

An old stage actor, Frank Dane, who grew up near Marshalltown, Iowa, told me about how he left the farm. His story summed up all the exasperation and frustration of plowing corn with a team. "It was hot, the horses were fighting flies, and when I came to the end of a row about ten o'clock in the morning, I said to myself, 'Francis, you've looked at your last horse's ass.' I tied the team to the fence, jumped on a freight train to Omaha, got a job with a traveling show, and didn't see the farm again for twenty years."

In spite of the discomfort that went with the job, I yearned for the time I would be big enough to plow corn with a team, and to have the same standing as the grown men who could handle such jobs. Jimmie Hartz, my neighbor and sometime playmate, had graduated to that level of competence. I was consumed with jealousy when he came by our house with his team and plow, condescending in his lofty way, to nod in my direction on his way to the field.

My fury did not alter the fact that my arms and legs weren't long enough to reach the handles and the stirrups on a horse-drawn corn plow. By the time I had grown big enough to do the job, we were farming with a tractor. Then, once again, the task of plowing corn with the more complicated rig was beyond my capabilities. I burned with envy of my friends who were trusted with what I thought were glamorous jobs. In the meantime, an unspeakably ignominious task awaited me.

When corn was laid by, it meant, in theory at least, that the corn was big enough to smother weeds in the fields. That meant, again in theory, that no further cultivation was needed. Fields were assumed to be clean and free of bothersome weeds when the time came for corn husking in the fall, only it usually didn't work out that way. Certain hardy bandits found ways to survive in the fields, making our lives miserable at husking time.

The worst were smart weeds (water peppers), thistles, Spanish needles, cockleburs and, especially, morning glories. I learned early on to loathe, despise and abominate the sight of morning glories. I cursed morning glories with the same fervor French farmers curse the pretty red poppies that litter their fields. Morning glories were special nuisances, winding themselves around the growing corn and choking it to death. They grow so close to the corn stalks that plowing them out is impossible; if you plowed out the morning glory, you took the corn stalk with it. Someone had to go through the field with a hoe or his bare hands to chop or pull the offending weeds. It was the kind of job that was given to a know-nothing, a dolt, a cipher, the kind of job that was given to me.

To this day, I can only shake my head in awe at human stupidity when I see window boxes around city apartments filled with carefully tended morning glories. People say weeds are the flowers God forgot, but I can't believe God ever had much to do with morning glories.

Pulling weeds in the cornfield was the lowest kind of stoop labor the farm had to offer. Working with horses, on the other hand, was something I enjoyed, and I did well. There was plenty of that kind of work for me during haymaking.

While the Sun Shines

My favorite job on the farm was cutting hay with a team of horses on a mower. I liked seeing the standing hay fall clean cut in swaths; the fields were bright green late in May when the first crop of hay was cut. There was a rich, heady smell from the newly mowed crop. I liked the neat, square corners you could make with the mower. For many years as an adult away from the farm, whenever I passed a farmer mowing hay, I had to fight back the temptation to stop and ask him if I could drive a couple of rounds. Now that horse-drawn mowers have all but vanished, I'm sorry I didn't do it when I had the chance. I still think mowing hay is a good way to spend an afternoon.

Making hay was a big part of farm work in summer. Like thrashing, it meant getting together several families to do the job, but putting up hay took less than half the manpower thrashing required. In 1933, we worked with four or five other families when we made hay. By the start of World War II, that number had dropped to two or three.

Today farmers bale their hay, or they chop it and blow it into a silo, but seventy years ago, hay was put up in the haymow loose, after it had been cut, raked and dried in the field.

If it rained while the hay lay raked in the field, the windrows had to be turned over once more, but rolling the hay around too much meant the leaves containing all the food value in the hay would break off, and be lost on the ground We nearly wore our hay out by the time we got it to the barn and up into the haymow.

After windrowed hay had dried in the sun for a day, or two at the most, it was picked up on a hayrack. Fully loaded, the top of the hay on the rack would be about as high as the second-story windows of a house.

Handling green hay was heavy work, and the amount of hay coming off the loader was determined by the speed of the rack as it moved across the field. It was important to keep the team from going too fast. By the time I was eight or nine years old, I was handy enough around horses, and I was sometimes pressed into service as a driver on the rack that was loading.

I took it as a special indication of trust to be allowed to drive a neighbor's team. Our friend, Everett Timm, owned a pair of small black mules, very lively and fast. One of the men who worked for us was afraid of them, and I felt pretty puffed up when Everett let me drive his mules. Fern Timm recently told me how much she hated those black mules. Knowing what a joker Everett was, she lived in fear that Everett's jokes and the lively mules together might lead to a disaster.

Loading hay wasn't too bad as long as the field was level, but when the ground was even moderately hilly, the racks rolled like boats in a swell as the hay piled up on them. The higher the load went, the more the motion was exaggerated. There always seemed to be some kind of macho competition going to see who could build his load highest. Showing off was a good part of it, too. Everyone worked at top speed. Worrying about safety was considered limp-wristed.

Up to your waist in hay, moving heavy tangles of it with a pitchfork on a high-loaded rack as it staggered across the field was an unenviable place for anyone uneasy about heights, as I most certainly was. During one haymaking season when I was in my early teens, Aubrey ordered me up on a rack, and we went tottering off alongside a barbed wire fence, with the load built up pretty high. I had my mind much more on the fence below me than on what I was doing on the load I'm sure, and I managed to jab myself in the leg with my fork. I went to town for a tetanus shot with a shameful sense of relief. It never occurred to me to wonder what the rest of the crew thought about the man who happily left his place on the load, and drove me to the doctor.

When a rack full of loose hay reached the barn, the load then had to be transferred to the haymow. The device used to do that part of the job was also called a hayfork, but very different from the pitchforks we had been using. The one most commonly employed was called a "harpoon fork." Five or six times sticking the fork were usually enough to unload a rack, but it might take much longer if the driver didn't know what he was doing.

A nice balance of wet and dry is required when you are putting up hay. There is the danger of spontaneous combustion if hay that is too wet is put into the mow. Packed down tightly, green hay will start to burn on its own, just as oily rags tossed into a heap will ignite spontaneously.

With an innovative fit on them, Aubrey and Everett went out one day and bought a new-style hayfork. Nobody else had one like it, and it caused a lot of comment, not all of it favorable, by any means. Their new fork was a grapnel-like affair consisting of four heavy steel tines each shaped like a slightly closed capital "L." The four tines were slung from chains that ran through a central mechanism used to lift the whole thing. Loosely suspended on their chains, the four tines could be spread wide apart and thrust separately into a load of hay at any desired angle. With the new rig, they could take the full load of hay off a rack in only two or three lifts. The new fork was a great advantage when it worked, but it was a maddening puzzle to sort out if it happened to fall in a heap.

One of our neighbors, my good friend Earl Gode, had some colorful go-rounds with the new fork. Earl had an explosive temper that combined awkwardly with his limited stock of profanity. He showed great energy and enthusiasm when he was worked up, but his sulphurous comments were repetitious, one or two phrases over and over. His performance was sturdy and workmanlike, but it tended to be monotonous, nothing artistic about it.

Barns in the Midwest all had big hay doors at one end, on the second story, up under the eaves. Some hinged at the bottom and swung down, some were hinged at the sides and opened in the middle like casement windows, and others ran up and down in slides dropping vertically to open. These great doors had one thing in common; they could accept huge masses of hay.

Every haymow had a metal track up close under the peak of the roof, running the full length of the building. A car on the track was designed to accept the forkful of hay lifted into the mow, and to move it along into the barn. A long, heavy Manila rope was knotted into the end of the track by the hay door. The end of the rope was tied to a set of doubletrees with a team of horses hitched to it. My job was to drive the team.

I wasn't tall enough to harness the team when I first started to drive, but I could manage them well enough. I was eight years old, and driving the team was my first serious job on the farm.

The great, dark spaces of our haymows were spooky, but they were also wonderful places to play. As kids we climbed up on the beams under the roof, and jumped off into the soft hay. Haymows were dangerous places, too, because of the many holes in the floor through which we pushed fodder and bedding down to the livestock below. In our barn, two of the chutes for fodder were well marked by open frames constructed around and over them. Those frames enabled us to climb to the top of the hay store there, and they provided openings down which we could toss hay and straw.

It was the unmarked holes in the haymow floor that lay like mines awaiting the unwary. I was warned about them; they were pointed out to me; and from then on I was expected to know where they were. It was no problem when the mow was full of hay, but holes in the floor were a menace when the hay supply ran low, and they were only lightly covered over. Then it was easy to make a mistake, step into one of them and fall through.

It happened to me just once, but that was enough. A light layer of straw lay over the opening, the most treacherous covering because straw is so slippery. I was carrying a pitchfork, and fortunately it was still in my hand when I landed on my back on the cement floor below me. I say fortunately because, had I dropped the fork, I might have been impaled on it.

It was the first time in my life I had the wind knocked out of me. I was panicked but there was nothing I could do about it. I couldn't get up, and I couldn't get enough breath to speak. Aubrey was working across the way beside the horses' mangers, and my grunts and wheezes finally attracted his attention. He didn't ask, "Are you hurt?" He said, "I can never send you to do anything, but something like this happens." An odd observation, to be sure, since nothing of the kind had ever happened to me before.

On dark winter afternoons when I was sent to put down hay, the hayloft seemed sinister and forbidding. I couldn't take a lantern up into the loft with me because of the danger of fire, and I was afraid of the dark. I had seen the movie, Death Takes a Holiday, and I was convinced I was going to meet the dark shape of Death in our haymow. I had also heard stories told in our neighborhood of men who had hanged themselves in a hayloft, and were found there dead, dangling by the neck.

When we installed electric lights in 1939, they did nothing to dispel my fears. The small bulbs only glowed dimly in the vast, black cavern of the barn. I took care not to let Aubrey know about my fears. He had a knack for putting me to work at tasks he thought would cure my phobias.

No two barns were set up in exactly the same way, but as a rule the team pulling the hayfork walked along a path parallel to the long axis of the barn. The paths where I drove my team seemed always to be out in the blazing sunshine. It pounded down on my team and me, and flies harassed us impartially. Big blue horseflies stung like bees, and the little triangular "ear flies" were nearly as bad.

My horses' hoofs, with the rope and double-trees dragging behind them, soon worked up a thick layer of dust along our drive path, and finely pulverized clay, dried cow manure and powdered leaves from the hay rose in a stifling cloud around us. At neighbor farms, when the men got a beer-break, the host farmer always came by with a bottle of pop for me, and I took care to let my team drink at the stock tank.

The starting point for the team on the hayfork was sometimes a good way from the rack we were unloading, and often I could not see the man who was sticking the fork. I had to wait quietly until I heard him yell, "Go ahead!" Then I moved my team forward—slowly. It was important to move slowly because, if the rope twisted when the team was moving too fast, it only made a bad thing worse.

The hay rope itself gave us plenty of trouble. If the rope was new, it twisted and kinked and jammed in the pulleys, while an old rope might break under a heavy pull. I can still hear the rope creaking as it pulled taut, followed by the sharp pop, and the general chaos that came when a rope broke: the lifted fork-full of hay dropped back onto the rack, sometimes on top of the driver; my team, relieved suddenly of their heavy load, had to be stopped and calmed down; the rope, having run back through several pulleys, now had to be re-threaded; and, finally, the line had to be spliced. My friend, Earl Gode, was the only man in the neighborhood who knew how to work a short splice.

I watched him carefully, but he was fast at what he was doing, and I never caught on to splicing a rope simply by watching.

As the strain of the heavy load came on the harness and rope, the doubletrees, tugs and all rose up about waist high, making an unattractive prospect in the event of an accidental break. "That would likely cancel your posterity," was the way one hired man put it. For safety's sake, I walked well off to one side of my team.

One day the man on the rack saw the rope twisting, about to jam, and tried to free the line without yelling to me to stop my team. The walkway for the team that day was actually inside the barn. I couldn't see what was happening on the rack. John Bury, the man unloading, got his fingers wedged between the sheave and the rope, and the flesh on his first and middle fingers was stripped away in an instant. I felt terrible about it, thinking I was responsible for the accident, but the men on the crew, including John, told me I wasn't to blame.

If the fork jammed going into the car in the peak of the barn, I had to stop my team and back them, lowering the fork and its big wad of hay toward the rack until, with any luck, the rope came untwisted. It was hard to stop the team when they were pulling a heavy load, when they were "up on their toes," intent on going ahead. Backing them was harder still. I sometimes had to make several tries—moving the team ahead, stopping them, backing them and trying again—before the sheave clicked in and the car ran down the track to the men in the mow.

Mowing hay was a job usually shared by two men, working in the dust and the heat, keeping the hay that came through the big doors leveled off.

Having dropped a forkful of hay in the mow, the man on the rack pulled the empty hayfork back out of the barn with the trip line. The weight of the fork dropping down from the peak of the barn pulled the rope back faster than my team was moving, so I had to drive with one hand, and hold the rope in the other, lifting the doubletrees off my horses' heels. It was a little too much to expect of a kid, but no one seemed to notice that, and I wasn't about to complain. Doing my job well gave me some of the status I craved. I wasn't going to jeopardize that.

Some of the farmers I helped with haymaking, particularly Earl

Gode and Everett Timm, were good souls who must have remembered what it was like to be a boy. They always paid me a little something for my work, even though, strictly speaking, Aubrey was the one helping them, and I was more or less thrown in to boot. My friends overlooked that fine point, however, and paid me fifty cents or even as much as a dollar a day. I always hoped they would do it when Aubrey wasn't looking. Not that he would have taken my money. It was just that he thought I wasn't worth much. My wages sound pretty thin now, but you have to recall that back in those day before the war, Aubrey hired grown men for twenty-five, later thirty, dollars a month, plus their room and board. And they were glad to get it—at least they were until they got better acquainted with the old man.

Aubrey seldom taught me how to do anything, at the same time he was pleased enough to yell at me when I came up ignorant. He was willing enough to overlook the fact he hadn't explained something to me.

"Take a half-hitch around that post!"

(What's a half-hitch? Where do you put the other half?)

"Go harness that team!"

(Who showed me how to harness a team?)

At the time I got that particular order, I wasn't tall enough to buckle the horses' collars. When, like Mark Twain, I replied promptly and said I didn't know how, Aubrey's stock response, word for word, was, "You goddamned dummy, you don't know anything, do you?" Those words made a lasting impression.

Now, as I think back over my life on the farm, I realize Aubrey actually did show me how to do several things. The worst thing about him was his unpredictability. I never knew when he would strike out at me verbally, and his reprimands cut like a knife. When an adult took time to explain something to me, I never forgot the kindness.

We were making hay at Everett Timm's farm, and I was unhitching my team at noon. No problem about unhooking the tugs from the doubletrees, and hanging them up on the horses' rumps. Unfastening the reins and disposing of them was another matter. I had the lines undone, and was clumsily winding them around the hames, making a bird's nest of the job, when Everett's father-in-law, an elderly German named Weiss, saw me as I was struggling, and helped me out.

"Now, I show you how to do that."

He carefully pointed out which straps I should unsnap and where to re-snap the loose ends. Next, he showed me how to take the rein and double it, passing the loops through a ring on the collar, bringing it all up and over the brass knob on the hame, and pulling it down snug and neat.

I can see every move he made. I could still unhitch a team and hang up the lines if I had to. And Old Man Weiss has a special place in my heart forever.

Shave and a Haircut

There was nothing to do for pleasure on a farm; we went to town on Saturday night as a reward for the week's work. Even during the busiest harvest time, it was considered bad manners to keep a crew working too late Saturday afternoon. We got our chores done; everyone cleaned up—the mandatory weekly bath—we put our crate of eggs and can of cream in the back of the car, and off we went. Saturday night was the high point of the week for everybody.

On Saturday nights, all the little farm towns were lighted up; Marengo like the rest in those days. The parking spaces around the square were filled with cars from early in the evening. All parking then was, as it still is, diagonal, the cars nosed in at the curb, except that now there are parking meters all around the square. It would have been a rare soul who drove to town with a team, but there were still metal rings set in the curb stones where horses could be hitched, and on the northeast corner of the square there was a watering fountain for horses.

Stores stayed open until eleven o'clock or midnight. Sidewalks were crowded with people doing their shopping and gossiping with friends. It is sad for me now, having been away from my hometown for over forty years, to find the place deserted on Saturday night, only a tavern and a pool hall open now, the streets dark and gloomy, and no one in sight on what had been our big night out.

In the years before the war, we had Saturday night band concerts in the park during summer months. The bandstand was set a little off-center in the southwest quadrant of the town square. It was octagonal with green painted wooden benches built inside a cement block balustrade, the seating supplemented by folding chairs for musicians who couldn't be accommodated on the benches. Kids from toddlers to about ten years old stood in ranks on the steps of the bandstand to get a good, close look at what was going on. The overflow hung onto the outside of the balustrade, peering over the shoulders of the instrumentalists.

Our town band, as I first remember it, was a mix of townspeople and high school students. We had a mildly eccentric electrical repairman and general handyman in town named Duffy Bishop. The tall antenna he put up for ham radio transmission is still standing on the lot where he lived in the east end of town. The whole Bishop family performed with the town band. Duffy himself thumped the bass drum; his wife, Maude, puffed away at a tuba; and his daughter, Helen, played the Sousaphone.

Dick Bryant was bandmaster, a tall, slender man with a hairline moustache. He played the trumpet, a beautiful gold instrument with an engraved bell and a ruby mouthpiece. When the night's offering required a trumpet part at the opening, Bryant gave the downbeat with his instrument at his lips.

Many people spoke highly of our bandleader. I knew him slightly, but I never saw him smile or heard him laugh. Dick Bryant taught music at Marengo High School, where he had a reputation as an excellent musician among his students, the kind of approval not easily come by when you are a hometown man working with high school kids.

Bryant gave up teaching after the war, perhaps because of the wretched pay. Without a leader, our Saturday night band concerts passed into history, and a happy feature of life in town was lost.

Across the street west of the bandstand was Marengo's picture show, the Strand, where the bill changed three times a week. On Friday and Saturday, we had cowboy shows and detective stories. Romantic comedies were presented on Sunday and Monday, while Tuesday, Wednesday and Thursday were the nights when we had big, lush productions—melodramas and historical pieces.

Admission was a dime for kids under fourteen. Adults and adolescents big for their age had to pay a quarter. I was a runt, and I got away with paying ten cents until I was a junior in high school. Then I decided to go straight and paid the full fare.

Some businesses in town advertised with colored slides flashed on the screen before the program started. The slogan for the Greeks' Candy Kitchen was, "Sweets for the Sweet." There were previews and newsreels to begin, then the main attraction, always a single feature, followed by a comedy or a cartoon. The complete program lasted around two hours. The entire evening's presentation was repeated a second time each night. If you really wanted your dime's worth, you could go in at seven, see it all twice, and be out before midnight. I learned the hard way that my parents considered near midnight to be too late for me to keep them waiting. From then on, staying through the second show was a risk I took only when the reward seemed too great to resist.

The ticket booth for the Strand was centered under the marquee. Posters for coming attractions were displayed on the walls around it, and on a sandwich board out in front. If the manager left the ticket office door into the lobby open for ventilation, you could see the screen from outside. Kids who didn't have a dime to get in, or who were making hard choices about how to spend the only ten cents they had, could chisel a little and see the show for free. It was just a matter of ignoring the glares of the manager and craning past him to see the screen. There was no sound, of course, but you can follow movies well enough without sound. Ernie Bell and I scared ourselves stiff watching *The Bride of Frankenstein* that way.

Inside the Strand a center aisle ran between twenty or twenty-five rows of seats.

At one time there had been a usher with a flashlight who guided patrons to their seats, but that posh touch vanished with the war. Kids liked to watch the show from the first row in front. Whenever there was an untoward racket, it came from the front of the house.

There was an emergency exit on the left-hand side at the front of the auditorium. When the show was crowded and the usher was distracted taking tickets, it was possible to sneak in through the exit door without paying, but that was a chancy business, hardly worth the dime you saved. The only emergencies we ever had were the minor demands of nature. There were no rest rooms at the Strand, and the convenience of the emergency exit was a convenience for men and boys only. Fundamentally we were politically incorrect.

As to parental guidance regarding what we should or should not see, there was none, or next to none. My mother used to reassure me that the show was "only a story, not anything real." That caveat notwithstanding, I was scared into fits by *I was a Prisoner on a Chain Gang*, *Death Takes a Holiday* and *China Seas*, but I never missed the smallest part of them. Only when *Gone with the Wind* came to town was there any serious discussion among parents as to whether or not pre-teen boys should see it. I don't know what they did about pre-teen girls. The red-hot love scenes, of course, were the central concern. Murder and mayhem were acceptable; human passion was not.

The Strand was owned and operated by a couple named Panknen. Otto Panknen died in early middle age, and his widow, Ida, carried on running the show, but the load may have been too much for her. She suffered from some mental disorder that overcame her periodically, causing her to display the most bizarre behavior, a gamut of oddities ranging from merely applying her make-up in a garish manner to screaming obscenities and trotting out into the street stark naked.

The State of Iowa mental hospital at Mount Pleasant was a medieval institution—there was no other word for it. I had to visit the place once as an assignment for a college psychology class. It was like something painted by Hogarth.

Ida would be sent away to Mount Pleasant for a while, and later she would re-appear, her old self once more. People used to say, "When Otto was alive he could handle her." Whether or not that was true, Ida's behavior didn't change much until she met and married a small-time hustler named Jack Gibbs who drifted into our community.

Gibby was a hale-fellow-well-met sort, a glad hander who fit well enough into what passed for social life in Marengo. He seemed to be genuinely fond of Ida. It was obvious to everyone that she was his meal ticket, but he looked out for her, and nobody thought the grief he showed when she died was less than genuine. A few years later, when Gibby, too, passed away, they buried him in the Panknen lot, Otto and Ida next to each other under the big family stone, and Gibby marked by a smaller stone off to one side which is about where he had always been.

Ida and Jack Gibbs had tried to keep the Strand in some kind of repair, but during the war materials were hard to come by; things got ahead of them and then the place ran down badly. One symptom of decline was an increase in the rat population at the picture show.

My mother had a phobia about rodents. Mice made their home in our battered old V-8, and I may just tell you it was worth your life to be in the car when Maude was driving and a mouse poked his head out of the hole beside the brake lever.

Maude knew the Strand was rat-infested, and one night while she and Aubrey were at the show, the handle of a purse she was holding on her lap dropped over and struck her on the knee. In a voice modestly low, but charged with genuine emotion, she said, "Oh, my God, Aubrey," loudly enough that people sitting near them were immediately interested. My father, who had been keeping an eye on a rat maneuvering up and down the aisle, but not saying anything about it for the sake of peace, decided they might as well go home.

About ten thirty or eleven o'clock on Saturday nights, the Sunday edition of the Des Moines Register arrived in Marengo on the truck delivering cans of film for the next day's picture at the Strand. Jimmie Lonergan and I lay in wait, grabbed the bundle of papers and ran off with them to Ray Lindsay's soda fountain, the only place in town selling Sunday papers. Ray was my pal's uncle. One of his legs was about six inches shorter than the other. He wore a shoe with a kind of rocker device under it, and everyone but his wife called him Peggy.

Ray Lindsay's wife, Agnes, didn't really care much for kids, and most of us didn't like her, either. We certainly weren't disposed to give her the benefit of the doubt, not to the extent of spending our nickels and dimes with her, at any rate. Of the two ice cream parlors in Marengo, the Greeks' was our clear favorite. It was smaller than Lindsay's, not as nicely appointed, and pretty messy, but we liked it. So, after we bought a paper from Ray (ten cents for the Sunday edition) faithless scoundrels that we were, we took it around the block to the Greeks' Candy Kitchen where we drank fountain Cokes and read the comics in a back booth. Our favorite strip was The Katzenjammer Kids. We went to all kinds of lengths deciding who was going to get to read it first.

Down the block east from the Greeks' there was a corner stand run by a tall, dour old fellow who had to deal with snotty kids yelling for extra butter on the popcorn he sold. Inside his four-by-four booth he had a mechanical clown that never tired at its task of turning a little barrel-shaped peanut roaster.

One of Aubrey's favorite stories was about a fellow from Amana out on a date with his girl in Marengo one Saturday night. As they passed the popcorn stand, the girl said, "Golly, that popcorn smells good!" Her beau obligingly answered, "Gee, we just ought to walk by and smell it again."

In those lively times, Marengo had four barber shops: Louis Payne ("Shave with Payne" it said on his window), Earl "Puggy" Myers, Cliff Jenkins, and Louis Colson all did big business on Saturday night, with their shops full of men waiting their turn for a shave and a haircut. Women weren't exactly excluded, they just didn't go to barber shops much. They had their beauty parlors where there were no men in sight.

Getting a shave in town was the only sensuous pleasure legitimately available to men. For a few minutes, battered farmers could enjoy the luxury of stretching out in the barber's chair with hot towels on their faces and somebody attending to them for a change. Pampered and powdered, they came away trimmed up, slicked up and smelling like several different roses, all for less than a dollar. It was definitely worth the trip.

Odd Fellows' Cemetery
1991

From the crowd around Morey's open grave, I craned my neck to look over at my grandparents' family lot. It was a cold, ugly day. My grandma liked clear blue skies. Once when I was still a little kid I told her how pretty I thought the sky was when it was full of white clouds, floating from horizon to horizon like a herd of sheep. She said she liked the sky best when there were no clouds at all. Later I realized that she had dealt with plenty of clouds during her long life.

The author (*l.*) and Pop

Mom and Pop

My grandparents' pretty gray house was set on a large corner lot. A sidewalk slanted in at a forty-five degree angle from the main walk in front. The yard was big—there was grass to cut with a push mower, leaves to rake and walnuts and butternuts to pick up from trees that grew in the yard. Old Mr. Rabe, short, fat, and grumpy, who lived down the block, came by with his cane swatting stray walnuts off the walk, afraid he'd fall if he stepped on one of them.

Big bushes of bridal wreath grew on the front parking, and at the side of the house. There were violets and jack-in-the-pulpit growing close in around the front porch. In back, near the barn, there was a circular tulip bed. In the fall of the year, Pop and I raked up great piles of leaves from the soft maple trees in the yard. We banked some of them around the house against the winter cold, tacking them in place with thin slats of wood over tarpaper. The rest we burned out in the road on the east side of the house. Today, the sweet smell of burning leaves is called pollution, and no one is allowed to dispose of them in a fire, one of the ways we've progressed toward a better world.

Before the pesticides of the '50s decimated them, summer evenings were lighted by fireflies that rose from the grass and bushes in winking, glittering clouds. We caught them and killed them rashly in bottles and jars with no thought of the beauty of what we held in our hands.

Pop put the American flag up on the front porch on the Fourth of July and Memorial Day—then called Decoration Day. That was the day we took flowers out to the cemetery, the good old standbys: iris, peonies, and bridal wreath.

Their cemetery lot had an iron urn in which live flowers could be planted. Getting the urn cleaned out and replanted each season was an annual task. The lot also had a tall pine tree growing on it. Today both the tree and the urn are gone, and Mom and Pop sleep in the shade of trees from in their neighbors' lots.

In the days before air-conditioning, the screened-in back porch was a lovely place to eat in summer, with temperatures on their way to 85 or 90 degrees by eight o'clock in the morning. People who needed ice in the summer used a card with large numbers—25, 50, 75, 100—printed around the edge. You set the card up in your kitchen window with the amount of ice you wanted at the top, and the iceman carried that size chunk in on his back, putting it into the icebox as part of his service. Kids rallied around the truck to grab slivers of ice that broke off the blocks.

We didn't lock our doors on the farm, but in town, my grandma and my aunt never left the house without carefully locking both doors—wicked-city syndrome, I guess. They tucked the front-door key under a flat, gray stone that they also used to hide whatever money was due to the milkman and the paperboy. Their back door key hung in plain sight from a nail driven into the molding. Both doors had locks that were stiff and balky, and it took an expert to open either one, whether you had the key or not.

A small entry separated the front door from the interior of the house. The front hall was always chilly, even in summer. The brass front door knob was a little loose on its shaft, and the front door had a tendency to bind. The glass window rattled and shivered in its frame when the door was opened. Once past the rattle, you met the smell of cold linoleum, cigar smoke and varnished wood.

My grandma's kitchen had taps for running water, but she also had a pump at the sink for soft rainwater from a cistern below. Over the sink there were two windows that opened to the side—casement windows. That sounds rather grand, but those windows were anything but grand. Mom could pitch her voice high when she needed to, and her way of calling me home when I was out playing with my friends in the neighborhood was to open the kitchen windows and sing out for me. I could hear her, "Diiiiiick!" three or four blocks away. It was downright unsettling to have one of the gang warn me when I hadn't heard her, "Your grandma's calling you." It meant trouble if I didn't stop whatever I was doing that instant, and leg it for home.

My grandpa put up a small shelf in the dining room to hold his Westminster chime clock. The clock made a tiny clicking noise when it was about to strike the hour. No sound was lost in the quiet of a Marengo night. I could hear that click when I was upstairs in bed, just as I could hear the switch engines working down at the depot eight blocks away. Today, in New York, I can hardly hear the clock ticking when I put my ear against the case.

Furniture in the front room was set up around the stove. We gathered there for warmth. That sounds poverty-stricken, but we thought it was friendly and cozy. The room always smelled of Pop's cigars. My grandma groused about it, but, after Pop died, I think she missed it. I know I did.

Newspapers ran evening editions in those days. My grandpa subscribed to an evening paper, the *Davenport Democrat*, with a comic strip I especially liked, *Highlights of History*, about Daniel Boone and Davy Crockett.

There was a backroom on the first floor they called the library, because it once held a writing table and some bookshelves. An Edison record player was tucked into one corner of the back room, a cabinet model with disc records about a quarter of an inch thick standing on edge in slots in the base. My favorites were "On the Road to Mandalay" and "The Field Artillery March." There were a couple of comic numbers, too, "Scandinavia" and "The Darktown Strutters' Ball."

The stairway in my grandparents' house ran twelve steep steps up to the second floor. Risers on the steps must have been about nine inches, with treads no more than seven inches. Going up those stairs was like climbing a ladder. I'm sure I could still do it with my eyes shut, as I often did back then when I came home late at night. Toward the end of her life, after my grandpa died, Mom had a bed made up on the first floor, so that she wouldn't have to climb those steep steps.

The house had no central heating. In cold weather, space heaters were put in the living room and dining room. A hard-coal burner, using clean but expensive anthracite coal, heated the front room. It had an elaborate nickel-plated device on top that could be swung aside to reveal a plate on which to heat a kettle of water. The door on the front of the stove had little windows of isinglass or mica. You could see the flames inside.

Marjory Simmons, nicknamed Madge, was a tough, merry, blunt-spoken woman with a clear eye and a ready tongue. Touchy and quick on the trigger, her entire life was a demonstration of what it meant to soldier on in the face of adversity.

Mom did a lot of sewing and mending, part of her regimen of thrift. She didn't bother with small patches. When she mended my overalls or jeans, she sewed a solid panel of cloth the full length of the leg. It eliminated the patched look, it was substantial and God knows it was warm.

Mom kept some of her materials for sewing and mending in a Fanny Farmer candy box she stowed in one of the drawers of her Singer. On one end of the box there was a picture of the Statue of Liberty. When I asked her what it was, she said, "That's the Statue of Liberty, lighting the world,"- which also happens to be the slogan printed on the end of the box. She told me that my grandpa had visited New York, and that he had climbed to the top of the Statue. Years later, when I was in New York for the first time, the one thing I really wanted to do was to go to the top of the Statue of Liberty.

"You'll eat a peck of dirt before you die!" was my grandma's battle cry when she thought she was feeding someone too finicky, very often me. It was a long time before I understood that the dirt I was going to have to eat was dirt I'd made for myself. Mom spoke with authority, having packed away her full share and more of the world's grit during her long life.

Mom moved fast, slamming her way through her chores with little regard for fine points. My mother used to say Mom braided her hair so tightly she couldn't shut her eyes. The daughter of the Evans family down the street who fell into my grandma's hands when her own mother was sick put it another way, "When Madge finished braiding my hair, I thought I'd never get my feet down."

She had a trick of opening the oven door on the kitchen range with her foot, carrying an unbaked pumpkin pie in each hand. Inevitably, the day came when the machine paid off; she slipped and spread pumpkin pie mix all over the kitchen walls and ceiling.

My grandma was an excellent cook, working as most good cooks do off the top of her head without recipes. Later, when she was older and had fewer people to cook for, she got out of practice, and some of the things she put together required real love and devotion to swallow, but that was only at the very end of her life. In her prime, she could whack the head off a chicken with her hatchet, pluck it and draw it almost as fast as I can write about it. She prepared her chicken in gravy, farm-style. Before I went away to the Service, I had never heard of southern-fried chicken, and when I first tasted it I couldn't understand what all the fuss was about. It certainly didn't compare to my grandma's chicken anyway.

When Mom made cookies or doughnuts she regularly made more than she needed, probably out of habits formed when she had three daughters to feed. She passed any extras around to her friends in the neighborhood. I was three or four years old when she handed me a bag of doughnuts, plus one for running the errand, to take to her friend Mrs. Rabe, who lived at the other end of the block.

The McBride family lived across the street west of Mrs. Rabe. They had a dog called Bob, a dog of no particular ancestry. Bob McBride was a big old fellow, and I was a little kid so we stood about eye to eye. Bob walked up to me that day, as calm and polite as you please, gently took my doughnut and swallowed it in one gulp. Mom dried my tears and gave me another doughnut, but I never felt quite the same about Bob McBride after that.

Mrs. Rabe would have been perfect in a vaudeville sketch as the wife of a stage Dutchman. In fact I think, had anyone put a character like her on the stage, it would probably have been rejected by the critics as overdrawn. Mrs. Rabe was a little less than five feet tall, as broad as she was long, chubby and ruddy like a Hummel figurine. Her comments on the world were prized all around the neighborhood. She sang in the choir of the German Lutheran Church where her efforts were taken to be serviceable at best. She knew her own quality, and she used to say, as wistfully as possible for her, "I think it so sweet, and it comes out so rotten."

As in most of the older homes in Marengo, electrical service in her house consisted mainly of ceiling drop cords. When Mrs. Rabe finished pressing her laundry and put her iron away, she disconnected the cord up at the socket rather than at the iron so that she could get the electricity left in the cord.

Mrs. Beulow, one of her friends, complained that their Lutheran minister was making excessive demands on his congregation, soliciting money for the church, "I can't give so much, I just can't." "Well,"

Mrs. Rabe observed," if you can't, you can't, and God knows you can't. But if you can, He knows it, too."

The Callahan sisters, Mary and Nell, lived across the street, east from my grandparents. They had once owned a farm north of the river, and they carried on doing a bit of farming after they came to town, raising a few chickens in a coop next to the barn behind their house, and gardening in their long cotton dresses and sunbonnets.

They owned a Model-T Ford. Mary did the driving. Like most people with Fords, Mary had taught herself to drive. The Model-T seems to have been designed to make a jerky start with neck snapping lunges as they moved off. Later, Mary bought a new 1936 model Ford. The new car had a stick shift, of course, but the old Model-T was obviously unwilling to release its grip on Mary's psyche. When she set out in her new V-8, she jerked it just as hard as she had the old car.

Mary and Nell, along with their neighbor, Mary Stone, were devout Catholics, faithful attendees at every Mass. Pop, seeing them set out for their devotions, unfailingly dressed in black, called them The Three Graces. Their homes were always open to visiting nuns. Knowing first hand what awful cooks Mary and Nell were, I assumed the nuns earned time off Purgatory for having endured the Callahans' food.

The last time Mom made a special treat for me it was an apple custard pie, one of her best creations. As always, she watched me closely for my reactions as I gobbled down my pie. When I cut the crust for a final bite, a stove bolt turned up under my fork. She had given the oven door her usual slam, and the bolt, loosened over the years, had shot out and into the pie where it baked just under the surface. I tried to cover my laugh by asking, "What's this, Mom?" I'll never forget the look of exasperation, combined with her efforts to keep her face straight, as she snapped, "Well, naturally, you'd be the one to get that piece!"

Pop was slim when he was young, with a full head of hair and a walrus moustache. He lost his hair before he was twenty years old, later claiming it was because he had worn a cap that was too tight during a brief period when he drove a horse car in Minneapolis. All his life, he liked to dress up and strike a pose, and he refused to blend in with the crowd in any group photograph. If the gang was looking east, Pop looked west. There were two constants in photos of my grandpa: one was his cigar, present in all but the most formal poses, and the other was a stern expression.

Pop started his life with nothing, but he had worked hard, and he managed to establish his own clothing store in Marengo. I have a dim memory of his store—the new-clothes smell, the hat rack that swung out of its space on one wall, and my grandpa waiting on customers with his vest unbuttoned and a tape measure around his neck.

Along with his many good qualities, Pop had a weakness for booze and pretty women, and that probably put him out of business. Maybe he didn't see what was happening, or maybe it was plain self-indulgence. The hard fact was that Pop and the entire country were down and all but out at the same time. After he lost his store, Pop worked at whatever he could find, even selling Fuller brushes from door to door.

Pop served as town marshal in Marengo for a while, a position that gave me considerable prestige with my friends around town. He had a policeman's cap he never wore, but that I liked to try on, a badge he wore on his belt, a pistol and a couple of saps he kept in the top drawer of the dining room buffet—the 'side board,' things that were forbidden to me, and therefore fascinating.

Taking me to movies where I didn't have to pay was a perk of another of his part-time jobs, one where he checked box-office receipts for Warner Brothers movies at theaters in towns around Marengo. I saw *Dodge City*, *Dawn Patrol*, *Robin Hood*, *The Sea Hawk* and *They Died with Their Boots On* so many times I knew the lines by heart. It's a wonder I didn't die of Errol Flynn poisoning. Pop sold me on the all-male movie *Dawn Patrol*, by telling me it didn't have a single girl in it, "not even a nurse," and therefore no sickening love scenes.

Pop was a great tease, and as an always-gullible kid, I was a hopeless foil for him. My stock birthday present for Pop was a box of cigars. His preferred brand was King Edward. The price was two for a nickel. If I squandered money on anything more expensive, White Owls, for example, at a nickel apiece, he quietly exchanged them for King Edward's.

I never really believed my grandpa would do anything to hurt me, but once when I was quite small, he asked me abruptly what I was giving him for his birthday. I balked at telling him, and when he said he was going to throw me down the cellar stairs, I yelled, "Cigars!" The family told me long afterward he had felt pretty sheepish about it.

Pop was always a great fan of my activities, but his devotion failed when a forward-looking English teacher staged Wilder's *Our Town* in Marengo in 1940. The play was first produced in 1938, so we were well up with the avant-garde when we presented it as an all-school play two years later. A year younger than the others in my class and short for my age, I was chosen to play Wally Webb, the small boy in the cast. Pop came to our performance, took one look at the bare stage with its folding chairs and pair of trellises, and walked out muttering, "That's not a play."

Two other traits set my grandpa apart: he didn't like dirty stories, and he wouldn't smoke a cigarette.

Pop loved fishing, and I pretended to like it, too, to please him. Out of his meager resources, he bought me a short casting rod similar to his own. I kept the rod and reel reserved for those times when Pop and I went fishing together.

Good worms for bait, nice fat ones, lived in wet earth under the broad leaves of burdock plants growing thick in the little pasture north of our house. They went into a can along with some dirt, and a pinch of coffee grounds mixed with the dirt kept the worms lively.

Pop and I fished together in the creek on our farm, and in Bear Creek west of Marengo, but the only time we caught anything worth eating was when we set "throw lines" in the Iowa River. Those expeditions involved staying overnight at a cabin owned by John Lindsay, my best friend's grandpa. The cabin smelled of dry logs, old comforters, fried bacon and wood smoke. In summer it was unbearably hot. Three of us slept on the ground in a wall tent, but Pop, who wasn't so fond of roughing it, endured the sweltering cabin for the sake of a bed and a mattress.

Throw lines were made from heavy cord about an eighth of an inch thick. They were from twenty to thirty feet long. A weight was fastened to one end so that the line could be slung out into the deep channel of the river. Horseshoes made good weights, so did the glass or porcelain insulators used to fasten telephone lines to poles and crossbars. Short lengths of cord, pieces a foot or so long, were attached to the main line at intervals of two or three feet. A triple-barbed hook was tied into the end of each of the short lines.

We used a foul-smelling dough mixture for bait, sticky enough to be molded onto the triple hooks. When we fished with single or double hooks, our bait was craw daddies, miniature lobster-like creatures seined out of the sloughs and backwaters near the river. We kept them alive in buckets or tubs with a bit of water, an olive-gray shimmering surface constantly in motion, making a faint clicking sound as the little beasts struggled over each other.

The Iowa River is a hundred yards or so across when it is at its normal level. For most of its width the river is no more than knee deep, but it drops off sharply into a channel where there is a strong current, and where the depth may be over a grown man's head. The channel shifts constantly as the level of the river rises and falls meandering among sand bars littered with the carcasses of dead trees and great chunks of river bank that have caved off into the stream when it floods. Sand bars increase in length on their upstream ends, shoaling gradually into the stream. Downstream there is a steep drop off into deep water, and that is where we set our lines.

The drop-offs on the downstream ends of sandbars are handy places to drown. I could swim fairly well, but Pop couldn't swim a stroke. The Lord must have had his eye on us, as well as on the sparrows, because we lived to cook and eat the catfish and bullheads we pulled out of the river.

We set our lines in the evening, just as it was getting dark. One of my several phobias, maybe a tribal memory of Welsh miners drowning in flooded coal pits or tin mines, is an awful fear of deep water in the dark. The stream where we fished in the black night terrified me, but I was too much of a coward to admit it, and I waded out into the warm, friendly Iowa River, sandy mud squishing between my toes, and my teeth locked down on the panic in my throat.

The Iowa River wasn't crystal clear by any means, but the fish we cooked and ate from that coffee-colored stream were white and firm, and they fried up golden brown. Pop was the cook. I have never since eaten any fish that tasted as good as those did, sauced though they may have been with the flavor of those long-ago times.

Almost everything about Pop was a little different from the general run. He saw to that, I'm sure, so while nearly all other Model-T's in the world were black, his car was gray. The last Model-T came off Ford's assembly line in 1927, the same year I was born. By that time, about seventeen million of them had been built and sold. Library shelves have been filled with tributes to that cantankerous but loveable vehicle.

In our safety-conscious age, it will probably surprise some people to learn that the fuel tank on a Model-T lay athwart the car under the front seat. Both the driver and the front seat passenger rode on a tank full of gasoline. Ford didn't bother to put a gas gauge on his cars until the advent of the Model-A, on which, incidentally, the gas tank was mounted up under the hood directly forward of the windshield. I can see Pop, a lighted cigar clenched in his teeth and the measuring stick in his hand, pulling the Model-T's front seat cushion away, unscrewing the cap of the gas tank and dipping the stick to see if we needed to stop at the next filling station.

Pop knew just how to entertain kids. With his scanty income, we went on excursions to the Amana Colonies. Old Grandpa Karsten had emigrated from Germany, the area around Mecklenberg and Schwerin east of Hamberg, some time in the middle of the nineteenth century, and Pop spoke correct German as his first language. He was a little snobbish about the gabbled German/English mixture used by people in the Amana Society.

When Pop had his clothing store in Marengo, people from the Amanas came to trade with him, partly because he was very easy about extending credit, but also because he could speak to them in their own language. The family used to laugh about a man from South Amana who came with his small son to buy new clothes for the coming year. Rural people shopped that way, buying ahead for a full year. They built up an impressive pile, and when the time came to pay the bill the kid said, "Hain't you gonna sling a pair of 'penders in?" So Pop slung in a pair of suspenders, and father and son went away happy.

The biggest treat of all for me was to go with Pop to watch the trains pull into the depot. We seemed always to go in the morning, and we stopped first to have our breakfast at the battered old River-to-River Hotel near the station. The hotel's name came from the River-to-River Road on which it stood, a connecting link between the Des Moines and Cedar Rivers.

My breakfast at the hotel never varied—a soft-boiled egg chopped up on toast. The waitresses seemed to know my granddad pretty well. Women usually had a smile for him, and for me because I was with him. When we finished eating, it was time to go across the street to the depot to watch the morning local arrive from Chicago.

The Rock Island Railroad is gone now, and with it Marengo's depot, painted a dull yellow-ochre, and trimmed in black. The name of the town appeared in block letters on a white panel at each end of the building. Semaphores, hand-operated from the stationmaster's office inside, stood midway between the building and the tracks. Tickets were purchased at an iron-grilled window protecting the sanctuary. Small boys were permitted to enter that holy of holies only with proper adult escort. Pop seemed to enjoy entry rights to all places, a privilege derived, I supposed, from some mysterious higher power. I went along gratefully, but with trepidation.

Depots had a characteristic smell, a mix of coal smoke, oiled wooden floors, re-lighted cigars, and hot, oiled metal. Today, when I stand on a subway grating in the city, I sometimes catch a whiff of something like that scent, tantalizingly close to the smell of the old depot back home.

The stationmaster's desk was set in bay windows, giving him a partial view east and west along the tracks. Between his desk and the windows were the big levers he used to operate the semaphores, but the great symbols of the stationmaster's arcane powers were his telegrapher's key and the receiver next to it. With no apparent effort—I could hardly see his fingers move on the key—the operator sent his messages clicking away to other stations far away up and down the line.

The telegraph receiver was mounted in a small wooden box, open on one side, and fastened to a folding arm that could be pulled out from the wall. A metal tobacco tin jammed in behind the receiver helped amplify the signal. Sir Walter Raleigh and Half and Half tins were best for the purpose. They were designed to telescope, the top half slipping down into the bottom, making it easier to finger out the last remaining crumbs of tobacco. Squeezed together, the tins fit neatly behind the instrument, and gave it a fine loud clack.

Notices to families who lost a husband, son or brother during the

Second World War came by telegraph from the War Department. Our stationmaster, a man named Hardenbrook, had to notify the families. People soon learned what to expect when they saw Hardy come up the front walk holding a yellow envelope. He hated the job, but he carried on with it, giving bereaved families at least one human touch in their grief.

A bunch of light canes bent into a big number-9 shape hung on the wall of the office. The bent canes were used to pass orders up to the engineers of express trains as they roared through town. A message on a flimsy-sheet was folded and wedged into the hoop. The stationmaster held the big "9" by its tail, and passed it up to the engineer as he leaned out of his cab to snag the cane on his bent arm, dropping it some distance down the track. There was fierce competition among those of us who hung out at the station to see who retrieved the dropped canes.

Steam trains went by fast with a blast of sound like a blow to the stomach. Contrast that to the stillness of a locomotive at rest in the station, steam hissing from escape valves, all its enormous power buried deep behind pistons, shafts and driving wheels as high as a man's head.

"All aboard!" and with a wave of the conductor's hand or lantern, the train began moving again. A series of sound-blows followed, great exploding chuff-chuffs, their slow acceleration sometimes broken by a rapid-fire burst of sound when the drive wheels slipped and spun on the tracks, the train moving off at last, its lights disappearing beyond a curve west of town.

Hardy's career ended on a sour note. He had an eye for pretty women, his job left him with too much idle time and one thing led to another. His last liaison was with the wife of a truck driver—frequently away from home. Hardy's wife was a good-looking woman with a fearsome temper, and when she got wind of what was going on, she contrived to tip off the trucker. The two of them appeared on the scene at exactly the wrong moment, pretty well putting a lid on the matter. I doubt that Hardy's wife and the truck driver knew the meaning of *in flagrante delicto*, but they sure knew what was going on when they walked in.

Pop and I could enjoy the excitement of two local trains a day, if we wanted to. A westbound train was due about ten o'clock in the morning, and the eastbound local came in sometime in the middle of the afternoon. Those trains may have had definite schedules, but they seemed to arrive when they pleased. Judging from the rumpus made by grumpy baggage car clerks supervising the loading and unloading, there might actually have been some intention of holding to a schedule, but the trains never ran on time. Pop and I took it all in, every detail, and then we chugged away in the old Ford to take care of other pressing business.

Pop was behind my very first grown-up journey. In the spring of 1935 he had some kind of political patronage job at the state capitol in Des Moines, and he invited me to visit him there over a weekend, if it could be managed. That meant if the roads weren't too bad, and if somebody could scrape up the price of a train ticket. I was seven years old, and the prospect of going a hundred miles alone on a train had me higher than a kite.

It was the spring of the year, however, and the roads were bad, and because our Model-T, like all its kind, ran partly on faith, everything stayed undecided until Friday afternoon of the day I had to take the train. Then my mother drove up to Aurora School to ask that I be excused early. I don't know where she got the cash for the ticket. She must have chiseled it out of her egg money.

They put me on the train at the depot late in the afternoon carrying a new cardboard overnight case I was careful not to let anyone touch, and I was off. Nobody bothered to tell me how long it would take to cover the hundred miles to Des Moines, and I started to sweat out my arrival about ten minutes after we left Marengo. It was dark by the time we made Grinnell, thirty miles west. I mistook the lighted dome of one of the college buildings for the Capitol dome, and I had my bag in my hand and was headed off the train when the conductor snatched me up by the slack of my pants and plunked me back down in my seat.

Pop knew exactly how to entertain a seven-year-old kid. The things he found to do were mostly free and always interesting. Early Saturday morning we were up and out on our way to the Capitol Building. In spite of the fact I was terrified of high places, we climbed all the way to the highest part of the dome. Pop cut off a splinter of the handrail—a considerable chunk of it was already missing—for me to take away as a souvenir. Later, down in the rotunda, we met one of the few surviving veterans of the Civil War, a white-haired old gentleman, who folded a slip of paper and, with one clip of his scissors, cut a five-pointed star.

We found Governor Kraeschel in his office on a Saturday, and Pop took me in to shake hands with him. Probably as a result of that meeting, Kraeschel went on to become United States Senator from Iowa.

Later that day, we went to see them print the Des Moines newspapers: the morning Register and the afternoon Tribune. In the shattering din of the pressroom, they gave me a copy of the Register, "hot off the press," and down along the line of rattling, clanking linotype machines, one of the operators kindly struck my name in lead type.

Across the street from the Capitol was the Iowa Historical Building. Saturday afternoon we went over there. The place was a kid's heaven, awash with Civil War battle flags shot full of bullet holes, muskets, pistols, sabers, plus Indian artifacts of all kinds. I remember in particular a buffalo skull with a stone arrowhead driven into it "right between the eyes!" We finished off the day in there, but I was far from having seen enough of it at closing time.

I knew Bishop's Cafeteria was the place to eat when you were in a city. Saturday night, we went to Bishop's for supper. On each table there was an electrified candle with a tag on one side that read, "For additional service." I didn't know what that meant, but I liked the pink light it gave, so every now and then I turned it on. I couldn't understand why a waitress kept coming over to turn it off, and I had to push some to drink all the chocolate milk Pop ordered for me every time the waitress showed up.

The combined bill for our meal was seventy-seven cents. That was when forty cents bought a special Sunday dinner—fried chicken or prime rib, stuffed tomatoes, creamed asparagus, along with dessert, hot rolls and coffee, tea or milk—at the South Side Café in Marengo. I remember the price of our meal because, when I got home again, my grandmother very uncharacteristically asked me how much we paid for supper. When I told her, she sniffed and said, "Well, you must have ordered everything in the place!" I didn't tell her I had nearly foundered myself on chocolate milk.

Sometime during the weekend, Pop and I had our picture taken together. A woman who ran the booth kept telling me to smile and show my teeth, but I had forgotten to brush my teeth that morning, and I wasn't going to let any stranger see them in that condition. All the other keepsakes of my first journey have been lost, but I still have that photograph of Pop looking serious with his cigar, and me with a tight-lipped grin.

I got back to school the following Monday a seasoned traveler with a year's supply of yarns to tell and curiosities to describe, giving me a leg up in any story-telling competition. It was true that the Ritchie kids had gone back to West Virginia to visit their relatives, but that didn't cut any ice where I was concerned. They hadn't done it alone.

Aubrey and Maude with a bumper crop.

Harvest

It was in connection with cutting grain during harvest that I had the sorriest job ever in my long life. I was seven or eight years old at the time. Aubrey was working with a four-horse team on the binder. One of them, Babe, the small mare with one good eye, was a slow, pokey old horse, and she couldn't or wouldn't keep up in her place with the rest of the team.

Among the junk in our shop, we had part of a McClellen saddle, a piece of equipment left over from the Civil War and named for the Union general who Lincoln said had a bad case of the slows. It was an uncomfortable thing to ride on because of a longitudinal split down the middle of the seat. The old man tied that contraption onto Babe's harness, and set me up in it with a hitch-strap in my hand and orders to keep the mare up with the rest of the team. He told me to use the buckle-end of the strap. When, in spite of the punishment I was inflicting, she lagged behind, he stopped the team, and yelled at me, "Goddamit, if you can't keep her up in her place, I'm going to whip you." I was more afraid of Aubrey than I was of hurting the horse, and I pounded her with the buckle end of that strap from morning to night every day until the grain was cut.

After these many years, I can't get the memory of that poor, suffering old nag out of my head, although I'd give a lot if I could. The witch doctors purporting to deal with problems like this say a resolution can be reached through forgiveness, but after I've forgiven my father for his brutality, and myself for my cowardice, what have I done for the horse?

At this time, I stood about as high as the ripening grain—in a good year, that is. To see the binder approaching pulled by a four or six-horse team was to watch the coming on of a mechanical monster. It was frightening, but compelling to watch. The big reel turning and pushing the stalks against the sickle-bar looked like an underfed steamboat paddle wheel. I could hear the sickle-bar chattering away, taking down all the grain before it, and I knew I had to stay out of the way of that deadly contraption.

Twine used to bundle grain was tough and hard to break when new, but it deteriorated quickly and lost its strength when left out in the weather. We bought our twine at the hardware store in town. It came wrapped in burlap, six balls to a bundle. Creosote, a tar derivative, used on the twine to give it strength, also gave it a strong smell. Like bailing wire, binder twine was put to many uses other than that for which it was intended, sometimes as shoelaces, sometimes as watch fobs.

Setting bound bundles up in shocks was the next step in harvesting. Sometimes there was a gang of men working behind the binder, or, when I was a little older, Aubrey and I did the job together after the grain was cut. Building a shock so that it would shed rain and not blow down in the wind took some skill, but not too much strength.

Nine bundles, including one for a cap, go into making a shock. You take a bundle in each hand, and ram them down butt-first into the stubble, slanting the bundles toward each other at the tops. Two more pairs are added at each side making a kind of extended arch, and a single bundle is set up on each side of the standing six. A last bundle is added as a cap with the heads of the stalks of cut grain spread out like a little roof, so that it will shed water. If the man working knew his business, he set the caps so that the heads of the grain were pointed into the prevailing wind.

Summer winds usually blow out of the south or southwest in the Midwest, so caps were pointed in that direction. Well-constructed shocks were supposed to be less likely to lose their caps when the wind came up. All the same, a common chore after a windstorm was to go out and replace all the caps that had been blown off.

I don't claim ever to have been much of a hand at shocking grain, but I have a happy memory connected to the job. Aubrey and I were working in the cool of the evening, and getting along well enough together for once, when the old man abruptly began to sing one of the old evangelical fox-trots, "Bringing in the Sheaves." He wasn't in any way a religious man, but he had a fair enough voice, and we shared a pleasant moment.

When grain had been left standing in the shock for a week or ten days, and was both dried out and fully ripened, it was time for thrashing. The very fact of harvest put most farmers in a good frame of mind, although there wasn't a lot of profit to look ahead to on any farm in the 1930s. It was always fun to have a gang of men around with everyone working together. Then they could see a tangible result of all their hard work. Exceptions have to be made for bad weather or insect blight, but at harvest farmers generally could look ahead to some gain.

Gangs of men working together seemed to be having a great time for themselves. There were no fights; arguments were friendly. There was a lot of banter and joking. All around people were smiling and laughing, no grim faces or dirty looks. Our sketchy technology did not eliminate work, but with many people sharing it, the job seemed lighter, even enjoyable. It was the kind of community endeavor and neighborliness that people still talk about nostalgically. Later, when combines did away with the need for big thrashing crews, I think people were in a way sorry for the change.

At thrashing time, farmers worked together in rings of eight or ten families. The size of the ring was determined by the length of time it took to drive home with a team after a day's work. People today, whose only knowledge of horses comes from watching the magical mounts in cowboy movies, don't realize that working animals get tired, too. While a team does often seem to know when they are headed toward home and steps off in a livelier fashion, horses aren't going to walk much faster than two or three miles an hour.

They tried to arrange it so that nobody needed to drive more than a half hour or so to get home after a day's thrashing. Rings didn't vary much from year to year. Farmers were conservative. Once an agreement had been worked out, it was likely to stay in place.

Threshing rings were set up around neighborhood families who owned and operated a thrashing machine, properly called a separator. Machine owners were paid by the bushel of grain thrashed. Payment in cash was preferred, but it could also be made in kind. Farmers chronically suffered from low cash flow.

The excitement of thrashing started the day before the separator was to arrive. Anticipation built up. Would they be here first thing in the morning, or would we be getting under way in the afternoon? In our ring, the work moved from west to east approaching our place.

The first sign of the big event was when empty hay racks came rattling by on their way to our grain fields east of the house. They would go out and load up, then come back to wait for the separator.

The thrashing machine came slowly up the road pulled by the same tractor that would be used to power it, carefully making the downhill turn off the road into the lot at the east end of our barn. Then there would be a big wrangle as the machine was maneuvered into place.

Our neighbor Jim Hartz owned and operated the machine we used. Jim had two sons, the older one named Maury, and Jimmie, about my age. We called their father Big Jim, and the younger son Little Jim. While Little Jim was too young to have any real responsibility on the machine, he basked in the aura of his father's ownership, and I loathed him for it. Our situation required that I be properly respectful, but I can't say we were chummy during the thrashing season. Maury, on the other hand, had a real job. He was the engineer, standing by at the tractor. Big Jim attended to the separator.

With Big Jim at the separator, and Maury at the tractor, the machine was started. They ran it empty—slowly at first and then at top speed, to make sure everything was in working order. Belt dressing, a black, syrupy-looking mixture, was dripped onto the drive belt to keep it from slipping, and Big Jim moved around the separator lubricating all moving parts with a grease gun. When he was finished, the rack loads of bundles were waved up to the machine.

Howling as it came up to speed, the separator chewed up the bundles fed into it from both sides. The racket was terrific. Working beside the separator, you couldn't hear yourself think. Some horses were too nervous to go up beside a thrashing machine. Farmers tried to hitch a jittery horse together with a steady one. Sometimes drivers had to drop out of their turn at the machine, waiting until they could put their quiet horse next to the noise.

A cloud of dust and chaff rose from the far end of the machine, the end that carried the straw blower. Big Jim got the worst of it working at stacking straw. He wore a red bandana knotted around his neck, but I couldn't see that it gave him much protection.

A medley of smells went with thrashing: sweating horses; sweating men, some clean, some not, in their work shirts and overalls, some clean, some not; the rubbery smell of the drive belt with its musky overlay of belt dressing; the sharp, clean smell of new straw; the rich smell of grain pouring out of the separator into wagons set to receive it; and the combination of dust and dried manure raised by the teams as they pulled their loads up to the machine, and then dashed away empty, headed back to the field to load up again.

I prowled around poking my nose in anywhere I thought I could. One safe place was under a pair of oak trees in the yard where we did our thrashing. Men waiting for their turn at the machine sat in the shade, leaning against the roots of the trees, smoking and gossiping. In good years we set out a metal silage basket full of ice water and bottles of beer, along with a few bottles of pop for the kids and the non-drinkers.

Another place where I wasn't likely to be chased away was the grain wagon parked beside the separator. It was an easy job, even for a kid, to direct the grain spout keeping the load of thrashed grain level, and warning the driver when it was time to bring up another wagon. One neighbor, possibly a little drunk, pulled a load of grain away from the machine without securing the tailgate, and strung a band of thrashed wheat across the lot where we were working. We scooped it up the best we could, but a strip of wheat later grew there anyway, a memorial to our thick friend.

As I got older, my first regular job on the thrashing crew was to help unload the grain wagons. We didn't have a mechanical grain elevator for some years. Grain from the separator had to be scooped into the granary by hand. It was a two-man job. I went as helper to the man who drove the grain wagon. We pulled up under a window in the granary, about shoulder-high as we stood up on our load of grain.

Two men unloading a grain wagon faced each other on the load. Using a scoop shovel, they threw to the right or to the left according to whether they were right or left-handed. They had to agree on rhythm and tempo as they alternated pitching shovels full of grain into storage. If you didn't settle the matter ahead of time, there would be some clashing of scoops, and somebody might get hurt. The agreement consisted in the older man setting the tempo, and me following his lead, especially when I was working with Aubrey. The pattern was dig, lift, cock and throw. Most people are right-handed, as I was, but I was also the junior member of the team, and I did not rate first choice about which way I was going to shovel. Instead, I learned to be ambidextrous using a scoop. I was determined never to break the rhythm, nor to drop out. Now, more than sixty years later, I am the proud possessor of an unmarketable skill—I can shovel either way, right or left-handed.

A typical thrashing crew in our neighborhood would likely consist of six or eight hay racks, each with a team and a driver, to haul bundles of grain in from the fields; four "pitchers," men with three-tined pitchforks who pitched bundled grain from the shocks up to the driver; a couple of grain wagons, each with a team and a driver, plus one extra man to help scoop; a couple of men who came with the thrashing rig, one to attend to the separator, and one to stand by at the tractor, the engineer. If the straw was to be stacked, another man might be there to handle that tricky job, although often the machine operator attended to it. Altogether, our thrashing crews numbered about eighteen men, give or take a couple.

The next big part of the job was feeding all those men. The expression, "He eats like a thrasher," isn't a joke. They consumed mountains of food, and when we moved to the farm in the 1933, thrashing crews ate not only their noon meal, but the evening meal as well at the farm where they were working. That meant the farm wife and her helpers put together forty or more big meals a day—they had themselves to feed, too, remember, plus any kids who were hanging around—and they had to clean up and wash the dishes and all the pots and pans that had been used in cooking. There were no mechanical dish washers. It was all done by hand.

Farm women toiled away in their kitchens with no air-conditioning, working over wood-burning stoves, or at best over kerosene stoves that still gave off plenty of heat, with no electricity and no running water. There were no prepared or frozen foods. Everything served at the table was made from scratch.

It is tempting to romanticize those times, and to imagine how good the food must have been, but it wasn't quite that way. Some of the neighbor wives were notoriously slovenly, and their food was so bad that marvelous feats of imagination were brought into play in developing excuses for not eating there, at the same time avoiding giving offense.

There were no effective pesticides in large-scale use before World War II, and with horses producing manure that fell where it might, we had flies by the wagonload. Screened doors and windows were black with flies drawn there by the smell of cooking. Passing through a screened door required it be given a couple of quick, short flaps to get the flies in the air, and then slipping in quickly ahead of the swarm. Women working in the kitchen shrieked, "Don't let the flies in." It was a wise kid who learned to cooperate.

Women tried to control flies inside the house using flypaper, gummy stuff made up in strips that hung from a tack in the ceiling, or in squares placed where food was laid out. They were soon covered with dead bugs. My mother said they were unsightly and unsanitary, they made her want to throw up and that was the end of the discussion. No flypaper in our house, no sir.

A popular brand of insect spray called Flit was advertised in newspaper cartoons, and their sales slogan, "Quick, Henry, the Flit!" became part of our vocabulary. Maude used Flit, pumping it out of a hand-held sprayer, but she couldn't do that when there was food on the tables.

Meals included at least two kinds of meat, beef and pork—roast or ham—often chicken, and the gravies that went with them. No meal went without mashed potatoes, some raw vegetables from the garden—radishes and green onions—and when the season was right, corn on the cob. There was never any kind of green salad; coleslaw was served instead. We were, however, presented with fruit and Jell-O mixtures in endless varieties. Pickles were a standard condiment. At our place, that meant pickled beets and beans. My mother had some strange bias against pickled cucumbers.

Maude seldom served pies to a large crew because she cut her pies into quarters, and baking enough pies to serve in quarters to a thrashing crew was too much even for Maude. Her cakes more than made up for it. There were always at least two choices, chocolate and white, the latter generally angel-food. Aubrey liked to put butter on his angel-food cake. I think he did it because it made my mother steam. Coffee and iced tea went with any meal. It was substantial food, there was a lot of it, and nobody went away from the table hungry, not even from the second table.

Eight or ten people was about the most any farm table could accommodate, even when it had been extended with extra leaves, so the crews ate in two shifts, a first and a second table. There was a subtle pecking order involved in sorting out who went first. Without anyone making an issue of it, the best workers, usually the most prosperous on the crew, were seated at the first table. It fell to the host's wife to call them in by name. The rest of the gang, and the kids, ate at the second seating. At least, the kids were supposed to do it that way.

Now, I confess I did my best to curry favor with my pals on the crew, hoping they would take me in with them to the first table. I could always depend on Earl Gode. Earl married late, and had no kids of his own. He called me Old Timer or Trooper and I had absolutely no qualms about Earl taking me in with him, even when I saw my mother slanting a warning look my way.

Feeding a gang like that, and cleaning up after they had eaten, was a serious undertaking for the women involved. It was altogether too much for one woman to handle alone. With choices made according to some exquisite balance of obligation and willingness, farm wives worked it out among themselves as to who did what for whom and when. The kitchen crew fed themselves in the dining room, but only after everyone else had been taken care of.

The old style of serving two meals a day, both dinner and supper, to a thrashing crew was an enormous burden for farm wives. The evening meal wasn't popular with the men, either, for the very good reason that it meant some of them would be getting back home to their farms around eight or nine o'clock at night. That might not have been so bad if there were someone at home to do the chores, but if a man came home late and had his team to take care of, cows to milk, and all his other chores yet to do, he'd likely be working until midnight. There were too many arguments against supper for harvesters, and the practice of serving an evening meal disappeared before the middle of the decade. You can believe the wives all heaved a sigh of relief.

Along toward the end of the 1930's, when farmers seemed to be a little less pinched for money, perhaps because of the approaching war, perhaps because of government farm programs, farm wives mounted a rebellion. The word got around about an arrangement that could be made with one of the restaurants in town providing harvest crews a substantial meal, and at a price farmers could afford to pay. I think some of the good wives added up their costs, and discovered it was less expensive, and a great deal easier, to send the men to town to eat.

One restaurant in town could accommodate a harvest crew on all points, quantity, quality, and price—the Marengo Café, on the south side of the square. You could tell when a harvest crew was eating there by the line of straw hats the men left out in front of the cafe. Today's ubiquitous baseball caps had not yet made their loathsome appearance, and there were hats of every description and in all stages of disrepair.

For some reason, God knows what, men thought it was funny to play tricks involving somebody's hat. Every crew had a character, the butt of all jokes. They set fire to one fellow's hat after he went in to eat. When he came out, his hat was in place, the ashes undisturbed and perfect. Then he tried to pick it up. The crew went together and bought him a new hat.

Carrying water to thrashers in the field was a kid's job, one of the things I was assigned to do early on. Some neighbors tried to avoid the upsets that came from drinking our dynamite alkaline water by carrying their own water in jugs from home. Others simply demanded that I get water from some pump other than the one on our farm.

I improvised a cooling insulation for my water jug, copying what I had seen done on other farms, by wrapping the jug in a gunnysack stitched together with binder twine, and then soaking it in water. The idea was to keep the contents of the jug cool through evaporation. It probably worked, but I guess nobody chilled his teeth on it. The going comment was, "Well, it's warm, but it's wet."

After Earl gave me his pony, Buck, I carried my jug on horseback. Riding bareback meant I had to do a little planning before mounting up. I wasn't tall enough to jump up on my horse's back unassisted, but had to mount from a stump or any available step. Even that was pretty difficult with a jug of water in my hand. Once or twice, before my legs were long enough for me to grip the horse properly, old Buck ran away with me, but I never fell off, and I never dropped the jug.

Maude hanging up the wash

Woman's Work Is Never Done

My mother had her own slanchwise way of looking at things. She liked to talk about a time when she could leave the farm, and open a tearoom. She intended to call it "The Scalded Pot." The pot she meant was not a cooking utensil, but that useful article for which there were several euphemisms: thunder mug, convenience, vessel. By whatever name, the slop-jar was an indispensable piece of household furniture, especially on frigid winter nights when a trip to the outhouse could be an ordeal.

Maude dominated the farmhouse. It was her territory. Out in the country they used to say you could tell who wore the pants in the family by looking at the house and barn. The one that got the paint belonged to whoever ruled the roost. Blessed were the homes where neither house nor barn needed paint. Without putting too fine a point on it, let me say that while our outbuildings sometimes needed attention, the house almost never did.

Maude was a year older than my father. I gather from things I heard her say that she had married primarily to get away from her parents' home, but I know absolutely nothing to support that idea. She went to Coe College in Cedar Rapids for a year, and she worked as a teacher for several years before and after she was married. People who were in her classes liked her, and said she was a good teacher, but Maude spent most of her life on the farm where she was obviously a misfit. Although she kept her house in the best possible order, she hated everything about the farm, and she never let anyone near her forget it.

Maude's special domain was the kitchen. That was where she spent most of her time. Farm families lived pretty much in their kitchens, just as today in city homes where the family room is really a kitchen.

We used our living room all the time, too. It wasn't like an old-fashioned parlor with everything in icy good order until some special event—most likely a funeral—put it to use. Still, we were most at home in the kitchen. That was where we ate our meals, Sundays included; my brother and I dressed and undressed there; and the hateful battles between my parents took place there. Family meals were neither leisurely nor relaxed. They were anxious times, the result of Aubrey's treacherous disposition and Maude's love of getting something started.

The central feature of the kitchen was the cook stove—a wood or coal-burning range. Ours had a reservoir on the right hand side for hot water. There was a temperature gauge on the oven door, very important for baking, except that my mother didn't trust the oven-door thermometer. She had one of her own mounted on a little cast iron pedestal. The warming oven over the stove was never used for warming plates at our house. We opened the warming oven doors and used them as shelves for drying mittens and gloves.

There was no sink in the kitchen. Wastewater was disposed of in the sink in the tiny washroom between the kitchen and the dining room. There were no special soaps for dishwashing. Maude used a paring knife to slice up Fels-Naptha soap, or she put slivers of hand soap into a little wire basket device that folded closed and could be shaken in the dishwater to make suds.

Laundry—there were mountains of that to deal with on the farm—was done in the basement where my mother had a pump connected to the soft water (rain water) cistern so she wouldn't have to lug buckets of water down the cellar stairs. She had another kerosene stove in the basement to heat water for her laundry.

Before the REA brought us electricity, Maude's washing machine was powered by gasoline. The engine had a kick-start pedal on the side and a flexible hose that carried exhaust fumes to an outside window. After repeated bending, the hose developed leaks. The characteristic smell of washday was a combination of Fels-Naptha soap, bluing and exhaust fumes from the gasoline engine. My mother was quite reasonably afraid for her life when she had to use gasoline indoors. It is a tribute to her good luck and her iron constitution that she never blew herself up or succumbed to carbon monoxide poisoning.

All the laundry was dried on a line in the back yard. In the coldest weather, I remember very well helping take down the laundry when it was frozen stiff, and of holding a pair of long johns out by the legs, rigid as a poker. In summer, the washing dried quickly in the hot south wind, but passing cars (we lived on the north side of the road) raised great clouds of dust that blew over the stuff on the line. My mother was convinced that anyone who drove past our farm and raised dust on washday did it with malice aforethought. Nothing could persuade her otherwise.

Ironing was a full day's chore. Maude kept the irons she used for pressing her wash in the warming oven over the range. They were called "sad irons." Anyone who has had to use one of them will understand the name. The Coleman Company advertised a gasoline iron, but it was expensive, $5.95, almost as much as we paid a hired man for a week's work. Maude thought Coleman irons were dangerous—a lighted stove and a little pot of gasoline sloshing around under her hand—and she wouldn't have touched one of them with the longest fork in the barn. Instead, she had a set of three or four sad irons, heavy pieces of cast iron shaped like toy battle-ships, blunt- pointed on each end, and about four inches thick. A metal holder fit over the irons. It had a wooden handle, and it locked in place with two little pegs that fit into holes in the sides of the irons. The heavy irons were heated on the top of the range. Maude picked them up with the handle, and checking with a moistened finger to see if they were heated enough to use. Judging the correct temperature was a matter of long experience and simple guesswork. On one end of her ironing board, she kept a pat of paraffin. She smacked the hot iron into the paraffin to lubricate it.

Before 1939, the house was lighted with kerosene lamps. One bracket lamp on the wall, another lamp on the warming oven over the range, and one on the table, lighted the kitchen well enough that you could read without too much discomfort.

The yellow light from the oil lamps made the kitchen look warm and cozy, bogus though that look may have been given the day-to-day tensions in our family. When Aubrey came in from work, dog-tired and frustrated after a long day, the least thing would set him off. Suddenly, for no apparent reason, he would start throwing anyone around him dirty looks, and snarling responses if you were foolish enough to ask what was the matter. My mother, with her Byzantine notions of how the world might be better arranged, never made any effort to avoid confrontations. Having raised the devil, however, she was then afraid to face him, retreating behind her barrier of tears and screaming, "Oh, Aubrey, you're so unreasonable!"

The wood we burned in the kitchen range and in the hot-air furnace in the basement gave off a white smoke that rose from our chimney straight up in the air on still, cold winter mornings. Walking through the woods, you picked up the smell of wood fires from farmhouses long before you could see where it was coming from.

Kindling for lighting the kitchen fires was kept in the wood box along with the regular fuel supply. The best kindling, and the easiest to come by, was clean corncobs, not those that had been trampled down into the muck. Some kitchens in our neighborhood were redolent with the smell of burned hog manure, but not in my mother's house. If the cobs I brought in were dirty, she sent me back out to find some that were clean enough to meet her iron standards.

Few farmhouses had central heating, but ours did. The furnace was in the basement. Most farms relied on small wood-burning stoves set up around the house during the cold season. In addition, every farm family owned a portable Perfection kerosene heater, a small enameled stove, about three feet tall and a foot across, with glass or mica windows through which you could see the flame inside, and a flattop to hold a teakettle. Perfection heaters were light enough to be carried from room to room. If you didn't keep the wick trimmed and wiped clean, they stank of kerosene smoke. Twenty years after leaving the farm, I found the same little stoves when I was living in Tripoli. The familiar stink made me feel right at home.

In winter, people either dressed at top speed in their bedrooms, or, more comfortably but with less privacy, in the kitchen beside the range. They piled on extra comforters and blankets when they went to bed. We put cotton flannel blankets on our beds in place of sheets when the weather was cold.

The heaviest work Maude did in her kitchen was canning vegetables from the garden, and "cold-packing" meat when we butchered a beef or a hog. During the early '30s, before my brother was born, and while she still had tremendous energy, Maude canned enough food to last us through the winter. Everything was put up in Mason jars she bought in town. Quart jars sold for sixty-nine cents a dozen, pints for fifty-nine cents. Lids for the jars were two dozen for forty-five cents, and "jar rubbers," the gaskets that went between the lid and the jar to make an air-tight seal—these were not re-usable, but everything else was—could be had at a dime for three dozen.

The first step was to be sure that everything was absolutely clean, a precaution against spoilage. Maude boiled jars and lids to make sure all bacteria had been killed. Then she filled the jars with vegetables or meat, added water leaving a bit of space for expansion when the jars were heated, put the lids on loosely, and brought the lot to a boil. She held the filled jars at the boiling point for a certain period of time, and then took them off the heat. Using towels to protect her hands, she screwed the lids down as tightly as she could while the jars were still hot. As they cooled, the contents contracted and the tight seal protected the contents. When you opened one of those jars, there was a hiss as the rubber gasket was cut and the seal was broken. That hiss told you nothing had spoiled.

Later, when the contents were prepared for the table, you had something that tasted something like braised beef, very good the first few times she served it. When you had eaten the stuff at least one, and more likely, two meals a day all winter long, however, it began to be an old story. The few guests we had always praised Maude's cold-packed beef, while the rest of us tried not to think about how much more of it there was down in the basement.

The filled jars were stored in our cellar. Maude never had anything go bad—a tribute, I'm sure, to her meticulous preparations. She had several quarts of carrots that stayed on the shelf for seven or eight years—we weren't so very fond of carrots, you see—until even Maude lost faith and threw them out unopened.

Before there were businesses in town that would butcher, cut up, wrap, and store meat in a deep freeze, we tried to share a beef with some one of our neighbors at butchering time. With no proper refrigeration, butchering was done in the late autumn when the weather was turning cold. Fresh meat was kept out on the unheated front porch to prevent it spoiling. It was always a worry, however, and Maude worked as hard and as fast as she could to get the entire portion of beef into jars before a warm spell of weather came along.

The worst part of butchering a hog at home was getting the lard rendered. All the thick coating of fat on the animal had to be cut off and sliced up into small cubes. The cubes were then melted down—rendered, that is—and the oil strained and cooled in one-gallon lard buckets. The smell of rendered lard stayed in the house for days. Some people claimed they liked the residue of the rendering process—the "cracklings"—and ate them like popcorn. They tasted like stale lard to me.

Most farms had a fifty-gallon drum for kerosene on a stand somewhere near the house. Ours was beside the backyard gate almost hidden from sight by a lilac bush. When the level of oil in the barrel ran so low that we had to tip it to get the last drops, Maude phoned in an order, and a little wizened-up Irishman named Casey came out from town with his tank truck to replenish the supply.

Since my mother hated the smell of kerosene on her hands, one of my chores was to make sure the glass reservoir on the stove and the two-gallon can for household use were kept full. Still, she got her hands in it when the time came to fill the lamps late every afternoon. I remember her saying, again and again, "If I just didn't have to fill these lamps, I could get my work done so much faster. If I just didn't have to fill these lamps." She probably believed what she was saying, but when we got electrical service, she didn't seem to have all that much more spare time.

Careful housewives—no one doubted that my mother was one of them– wiped away the carbon that accumulated on the wicks of kerosene lamps and stove burners, and trimmed the wicks smooth every day. That reduced their tendency to smoke, and it cut down on the strong kerosene smell stoves and lamps otherwise gave off. When you walked into a farm kitchen, one whiff told you how things were managed there.

Another mark of a good housekeeper was the condition of her lamp chimneys. They were supposed never to show fingerprints or smoke stains. Moviemakers today don't seem to know that lamp chimneys are supposed to be kept sparkling clean. Fine homes and palaces alike in period movies routinely display lamps with blackened chimneys looking like they came from some shanty back of the yards. Aubrey and some of our hired men had a trick of lighting their cigarettes over Maude's lamp chimneys. The first puff left a smoky stain as evidence of the nefarious practice. God help them, whoever they were, when my mother caught them at it.

Men working on farms in the summer came in from the field caked with dirt and sweat. The Saturday-night-only bath rule didn't hold in the summer months. There may have been people who managed with a bath a week in hot weather, but you wouldn't want to be around them much. With no bathroom and no running water, my mother filled two washtubs with water around the middle of the day, and dragged them out into the sunshine in the yard back of the house. The tubs were gray galvanized metal, dark enough that they absorbed the sun's rays, and so warmed the water. On a sunny day, the water in the tubs would be plenty warm enough to bathe in by evening, a practical use of solar energy long before anyone had thought to put a name to it. When it was rainy, or the weather was chilly, Maude heated tubs of water in the basement for the men to use. Privacy wasn't as much of a problem as it might seem. Practical people didn't look at what they didn't need to see—a useful practice on a farm where there was more than enough to turn an ordinary stomach.

Our hired man had his own room with a comfortable bed. His linen was changed once a week, the same as for the rest of the family. Maude kept her house bone-chillingly clean, and the men ate well. Within the limits she set for herself, my mother was a good cook. There was always enough to eat on the table. It was a meat-and-potatoes diet, but there was plenty of it.

Carrying the grinding load of work she did, Maude had no social life of any kind to give her relief. She didn't go to church; she didn't play cards; she belonged to no clubs. Reading and the radio were her recreation at home. Late in her life she became interested in antiques, and she took up painting, an activity that gave her some of the artistic outlet she always craved. Breaks in her daily labors came only with her weekly trips to town for shopping, an occasional movie or one of those rare occasions when we went to Cedar Rapids. She made no secret of the fact that she thought the world had used her badly, and by the end of her life her many excellent qualities were overridden by bitterness.

Doctors, "Ventinaries," and Other Violence

My first serious encounter with doctors—it was called minor surgery, but it was serious enough to satisfy my curiosity for all time—came in the summer of 1934 when I had my tonsils out and was circumcised on the same day. I was seven years old. You may wonder why this uncomfortable business was done so late. I can only say that I was born in Baylor Hospital in Dallas, Texas, where what later became routine was not done at all at that time, such as the circumcision of male infants. Whether that fact reflected enlightened medical views at Baylor, or merely southern lassitude, I have no way of knowing.

In the spring of the year when I turned seven, my tonsils had been badly infected for some time, making it difficult for me to swallow. Worse, the foreskin on my penis seemed to be growing shut. I accepted the decisions of my elders, although why they chose to have both matters attended to on the same day, I still do not understand. Surgery was presented as the sole option for conditions that would only worsen with the passage of time. There was nothing to be gained by waiting.

All surgery was then done under general anesthesia, and, in preparing me for the operation, my mother made sure I would not panic and fight when the ether cone was put over my face, and that I would not resist the effects of the drug as it was dripped onto the gauze. She made it seem like a game or an adventure—but she didn't say anything about whether it was going to hurt.

It all started well enough. I marched up the stairs to the doctors' office, and hopped up on the table. There was nothing about the place to worry me. The two old doctors, Brown and Patterson, looked just as they always did in their vests and shirt sleeves. It may be they kept most of their apparatus out of sight in order not to scare me.

I lay down on the table in their office, and did as I had been told—inhaled deeply, breathing in the fumes of the stuff they poured onto the cone over my nose. I didn't care much for the smell of it. The next thing I knew, I was sitting upright on the operating table. My first words were, "Oh, my peter! Oh, my pecker!" I heard somebody giggle. My small protest was afterward thought to have been very funny. They carried me down the stairs to the street, put me on the backseat of the Model-T, and we drove back to the farm.

They put me on a cot at the foot of the stairs in the front room, and there I stayed for about a week. My grandpa made a bed table for me that served double duty, kept the weight of the bedclothes off my wounded middle, and gave me a surface for my meals and my books.

Mom's sister, my great-aunt Florence, who then and later had an eye out for my betterment, chose this occasion to present me with an old, twenty-volume set of *The Book of Knowledge*. It had been published around 1910, and although out of date, it was full of a wide range of fascinating information, just what I needed to fill an otherwise boring interval. I can probably credit the later grab-bag quality of my mind to Aunt Florence's timely gift.

Many years after that, an Army doctor peering into my open mouth said, "Someone sure slashed hell out of your throat." It was the first and only informed critique I ever had on that part of the surgery. All in all, I recovered well enough, although it was a long time before I could tolerate the smell of anything that had ether in it.

If numbers were a true measure, we had more doctors than we needed in our town of 2,200. Doctor Hollis had his office in his home across the street east of the Court House. Doctors Patterson and Brown, and their nurse, Betty Clements, shared offices over Gode's Dry Goods. There was one more doctor in the spooky, vine-covered hospital that stood, dark and unused, across the street north of the town square, looking like the setting for a horror movie. The doctor there was the uncle of a high school chum of mine, but the building was gloomy, always empty. I was scared of it, and I never went near the place without a shudder. Perhaps there had once been a patient in the old hospital, but I never heard of it. There was no other hospital in town at that time. People went to one of the big hospitals in Iowa City or Cedar Rapids, or they died at home.

We also had a couple of chiropractors—a man named Dutcher, and a woman who went by the name of Spence, although her married name was Bates. Dr. Spence was a great favorite of my mother's, but I hated her with a passion. When I was about three years old, I came down with a severe respiratory disorder. My mother, in a panic, and I suppose short of money, called Dr. Spence. She treated me with hot packs.

I was tied into a high chair, and in one-hour sessions for three days running, the pair of them applied hot towels to my throat. Maude could put her hands into water that was near scalding hot, but the water they used for those packs was too hot even for her. I screamed my head off, begging them to stop, but nothing fazed them; they kept on with it. From that time until the day she died, I fantasized about how I would dispatch Dr. Spence should she ever fall into my hands. With the passage of time, my feelings toward her have softened, and I now think I would only have her burned at the stake. Maude always insisted Dr. Spence had saved my life, and that may be so, but she also bent my soul pretty badly.

Doc Patterson was very much a small-town doctor. He was genial, on the tall side, with a pleasant Irish mug on him. He knew enough to get by, and, so far as we were aware, he had never actually killed anybody. Boys my age got Doc Patterson to fill out the medical examination form for Cub Scouts.

Dr. Brown, on the other hand, was an interesting character. He was on the short side, and if he had been younger, he would probably have been described as burly. He looked a little like pictures of Benjamin Franklin. Because he was a keen diagnostician, Doc Brown was often called in for consultation by the staff of the University Hospital in Iowa City.

His daughters later urged him to write the story of his life, but he refused to do it. His reluctance to set down anything about his experiences was a great loss, I think. He had probably delivered half the population of the county, and performed kitchen-table surgery on a good part of the other half.

Doc Brown did some of the many surgeries our neighbor, Bernice Hartz, underwent during her life. After one such operation, Brown was getting his things together, but he couldn't find his hat. Everyone looked high and low for it. Finally, someone came forward with a hat so battered and disreputable looking they were reluctant to say it belonged to the doctor. Brown accepted it, and put it on with a grunt, saying, "That's my barn hat."

Doc Brown drove a Model-T. He was totally blind in one eye, and couldn't see very well out of the other, so it was a good idea to stay out of his way when he was on the road. He had an extra lens mounted on his glasses frame that he could swing around over his good eye when he really needed to see something. It was just as well, too, that he never drove more than ten or fifteen miles an hour.

Altogether, Doc Brown was a gruff, no-nonsense old fellow. When I was eleven or twelve years old, Maude decided I had better be inoculated against diphtheria, and she sent me to Brown. He looked at me, and said, "How old are you?" I told him. He growled, "You don't need this." And that was all there was to that.

When I was about eight, I went to Doc Patterson for a smallpox vaccination. It was an ordeal. Doc broke a little glass vial containing a sterile needle, and then he proceeded to make, slowly, four or five deep scratches—deep enough that they drew blood—on my upper left arm. He squeezed vaccine onto the bloody lines, and packed me off home with the thing loosely bandaged, "Just something to keep the dust off."

Back at the farm, I spent the rest of the day driving a team on the hayfork. The day following, I wasn't feeling so good. My arm swelled, I ran a fever and a thick, smelly crust formed over the spot. I still have a vaccination scar as big as a fifty-cent piece. Although I've probably been vaccinated a dozen times since then, and all of them "took," none was like that first one from Doc Patterson.

After Brown and Patterson died, a doctor named Watts came to Marengo. He opened a hospital in a big frame house on Washington Street across from the post office. Watts was not what you would have called a likeable man. He was short and stocky with an aggressive, big-city manner, a hairline moustache and a reptilian stare. He had half the town afraid of him, a fear reinforced by his only-too-obvious willingness to opt for radical surgery no matter what the problem. Watts' standing was compromised further in our blue-nosed community by the speedy way he divorced his wife in order to marry a sexy red-haired nurse. Peg Watts, the new wife, then immediately and enthusiastically set about building a reputation for infidelity.

My grandpa worked for a while as general handyman at the hospital. Pop always said he liked Watts, blaming the difficulties he had in collecting his wages on the doctor's head nurse, Dorothy Zuber. The two of them would get into fights about his back pay on the telephone, but they spoke in German, and the family was shut out.

I went to Doc Watts a few times for some trifle or other, to have boils lanced, to get a big splinter pulled out of my bottom, or to get a tetanus shot after I had punctured myself with a pitchfork. Knowing that he owed my granddad a fair amount of money, I never offered to pay him. A little cheeky for a teenager, I'm afraid, but it was my idea of justice, and, it's worth noting, he never sent a bill for any of it.

The day after Pop died, I was getting on a train in Chicago on my way to Iowa for his funeral. I met Doc Watts in the La Salle Street station. He had chosen that particular day to take a trip. Watts was, in fact, one of the very few people in Marengo not present when we buried Pop, but his son, Campbell, a doctor in Cedar Rapids, was there, just as he had been so often at my granddad's house during his last illness. More than fifty years later, Campbell Watts wrote me a note—I have it among my things—in which he said, "Richard, your grandfather was the finest man I ever knew."

Polio was one of the diseases we all dreaded. I don't believe anyone so much as thinks about polio now, except to have their children inoculated against it. It was called infantile paralysis because it so often struck kids. Every summer there was a fearful time when the polio came. We were warned to avoid crowds, and to stay out of swimming pools. The terror lasted until the first killing frost. No one knew why, but that seemed to put an end to it for the season.

In a family where going to the doctor was taken to be a moral lapse, the ills and sufferings of our livestock didn't get a very high priority. We seldom sent for the veterinarian—the "ventinary"—but on occasion, with an animal in extremis, we called Doc Gwynne. Gwynne was a good old man nearly stone deaf, and so short he could barely see over the dash board of his car, a Studebaker coupe with a huge trunk, "big enough to hold all my instruments of war and torture." Gwynne would come out to the farm, look at the ailing critter, and then tell us, "It'll be all right," or, "Knock it in the head." I never, so help me God, heard him say anything else. During the bone-poor 1930s, we paid him two dollars for that advice. The old doctor didn't approve of useless pain, and exploitation for profit wasn't his game.

If in our Heavenly Father's house there are, indeed, many mansions, I believe Doc Gwynne must have a nice one all to himself, some place where he can sit smiling on his front porch swing, as I used to see him in Marengo when I rode by on my bicycle, looking out over all the grateful animals he spared from unnecessary suffering.

God knows our livestock paid for it, but the brutal laws of economics made it necessary for us to manage our barnyard surgery on our own. The rule was use a sharp knife, and cut fast. It was hideous work. There was no thought of anesthesia for animals. It would have been considered outlandish even to suggest such a thing. For the most part, the tasks we dealt with were docking lambs' tails, dehorning cattle, and castrating pigs. Cattle have to be dehorned for safety's sake, and male hogs must be castrated so that they will fatten for market. Getting the lambs' tails off was by far the least bloody of these unpleasant jobs.

Sheep are not appealing creatures, and they stink in a way all their own. As to their dim brains, a good illustration is their sense of follow-the-leader. If you are driving a flock of sheep up a narrow lane, and you set a barrier across their path, the sheep will jump over it. But if you then remove the barrier, the silly creatures will keep right on jumping over the phantom obstacle.

The sickening smell of sheep comes mostly from the lanolin on their wool. Lanolin may be good for your hands, but, unrefined, it has an abominable smell, faintly resembling roasting lamb, and identical, in my opinion, to the taste of mutton. Still, little lambs have two endearing traits. One is a trick of bounding straight up in the air, seeming to leave the ground with all four feet at once. The other is, while being suckled by the ewe, their undocked tails waggle furiously. It makes chopping off those tails seem particularly mean, but off they have to come. Left undocked, the tails get fouled with excrement and loaded with maggots.

Lambs lose their tails when they are four to six weeks old. A hammer, an ax head and a block of wood are the implements we used for docking. Lambs' tails have a separation in the bone about two inches from the base of the spine. The blade of the ax is paced on the tail at that point, backed up by the wood block, and the head of the ax is given a smart rap with the hammer. A little diluted sheep dip is dabbed on the raw end of the stump by way of antiseptic. At least it's all over quickly.

Sheep dip is a powerful disinfectant that is mixed with water and put in tanks into which sheep are plunged, or dipped. This is ordinarily done after they have been sheared in the spring as a precaution against ticks. Sheep dip has a pungent smell. You knew without asking, even miles away, when somebody had dipped his sheep.

A special tool resembling a set of bolt-cutters is used to dehorn cattle properly. With one of those gadgets, the horns can be taken off or snipped off quickly and easily. The hard way is to cut them with a hacksaw, and that is how we did it.

The animal being worked on was locked in a milking stanchion, or its head was tied fast to a post while the horns were being sawed off. The pulp inside the horn contains both blood vessels and nerves. The animal suffers a good deal, and there is a considerable loss of blood. If the horns are just budding, not yet well grown out, the shock of the operation and the loss of blood are both kept to a minimum, but when the horns are well developed, getting them off is a gory mess.

Procrastination was one of Aubrey's worst faults, one I confess I inherited. He put off dehorning one white-faced bull until each of the horns was nearly a foot long and a good three inches in diameter at the base near the skull. The poor animal never really recovered from the shock of his ordeal. I remember him standing, as if stunned, in the barnyard with great streaks of dried blood on both sides of his head. He was never any use as a bull afterward, and he had to be sold for slaughter.

Castrating pigs, simply called cutting them, was the worst of our surgical enterprises. It is a two-man job, and, with Aubrey as the surgeon, it fell to me to catch and hold the victims. Hogs are intelligent animals. They could sense something unfortunate coming as we separated the males from the rest of the herd. As to my feelings about the unseemly task in which I was forced to participate, it is just as well that all I knew about Freud was his name.

Diluted sheep-dip again was employed as an antiseptic, although with the filthy conditions of our barns, I can't imagine any antiseptic powerful enough to do any real good. Having said that, I have to say we had only one fatality during the time I took part in the work. In that one case, the poor creature we castrated crawled into a pile of straw and died there, probably from shock.

Aubrey having assembled his equipment—a can of diluted dip, a whetstone and his castrating knife—a single-bladed pocket knife with a rounded tip instead of a point—he stood by with his hands dripping dip solution while I sidled as quietly as possible among the apprehensively snuffling hogs until one came near enough for me to grab it.

The job is best done before the pigs are heavy. I never weighed more than 135 pounds while I lived on the farm, and it was a pretty awkward business when the critter I was supposed to hold outweighed me. I grabbed the hog's right hind leg in my left hand, switched the leg to my right hand, grabbed the right front leg in my left hand, and flopped the hog down on his left side, holding him down with my left knee behind his head, and pulling his right hind leg up tightly, but not too tightly, taking care not to press too hard on the hog's side or belly, because my weight might cause a rupture through the incision.

Aubrey took the hog's scrotum between his thumb and forefinger and made a slit about four inches long. Then he removed the testicle, pulling the cords attached to it out at the same time. The cutting was repeated on the other side, and a little diluted sheep-dip was poured into the open wounds. The entire business, of course, was accompanied by hideous shrieks of pain from the hog.

We had a neighbor who used to drop by with a tin can to collect the spoils of our work. His family cooked and ate these "Rocky Mountain oysters," relishing them as a delicacy, a taste we did not share.

A while back, I read something about salt being used to cauterize wounds. I had seen that very thing demonstrated years before. One of our neighbors, a big, rough character named Everett Sleighmaker, had helped Aubrey slice a tumor the size of two fists off the ham of a hog. The wound bled furiously, and my dad complained to his self-taught surgeon, "That hog's going to bleed to death." Old Ev growled, "He ain't going to bleed to death. Gimme a bucket of salt." We brought him a pail of the coarse salt used to feed the stock, and he plastered it on the open wound. I was surprised that the pig didn't squeal when the salt went on. The bleeding stopped, and the hog survived.

The callousness and indifference to suffering farmers showed toward their animals all too often carried over in the ways they dealt with their own pain. One brutality spawned another. I am not trying to generalize from a single incident, but this story illustrates the point.

Our landlord, Tom Willis, had a terrible accident when he was a boy. He was blinded on his right side, but he didn't lose the eye. It wasn't disfigured, and you had to look closely to see which eye was the bad one. The accident happened during thrashing.

Tom and his brother Will liked to fool around more than they liked to work, and they had well-established reputations for getting into trouble. They had been running to see which of them could be first up on the back of a load of bundles. Someone had stuck a pitchfork down in the rear end of the load with the tines curving out between the slats of the rack. Tom was ahead, but he didn't see the fork when he jumped up on the load. One tine went into his cheek just below the eye, where it struck the optic nerve.

My great-grandfather, old Dick Willis, who migrated from England, didn't stop to get the details. He asked no questions about injuries until he had beaten both his sons with a rope's end on their bare backsides. Then they called a doctor. All this took place before the turn of the century. Anti-tetanus vaccine did not even exist, and everyone thought it was miracle that Tom didn't die of lockjaw. When Uncle

Tom told the story, he always quoted his brother Will, "I've got a 'O' on my bottom where that rope hit me yet."

Farm life was never the pastoral idyll people today try to make it out to have been. We lived with violence all around us—the worst of it, as I think back, was the abuse of livestock. It was an everyday matter, almost a casual experience. Farm animals were kicked and beaten with whatever was at hand—straps, clubs and whips. I watched while Aubrey lost his temper and beat a brood mare, heavy with foal, with the flat of a carpenter's hammer he happened to have in his hand.

At a state fair horse-pulling contest, it was a revelation to me to learn that the drivers were disqualified if they whipped their teams or swore at them. One driver who started to lash his horses with the ends of his reins pulled back just in time. The crowd laughed at his slip.

Men who took exception to brutality were regarded as eccentrics. Billy Sayers raised horses, and people said he made pets of them. One of the veterinarians in town—not dear old Doc Gwynne—complained that Billy was just too soft with his horses, so much so that the vet couldn't do his work, whatever the hideous chore of the moment may have been. They had to pack Billy off to the house in order that the vet and Billy's sons could get on with the task at hand.

Brutality carried over into the ways people dealt with each other. Iowa County's long-time sheriff was a dapper little man named Chris Englebert, brown and tough as whang leather. Chris had served with Pershing's cavalry during the 1916 Mexican border campaign—when they chased Pancho Villa all over the region and didn't catch him. Chris's wife, Rosetta, was a friend of Maude's, and I was often in their home. Hanging on the wall of their living room was a framed snapshot of Chris with a man's legs, one in each hand, cut off below the knee. The victim was a derelict who had been run over by a freight train east of town. You could see the picture clearly from their dining room table. I often wondered if they looked up at it while they were eating.

Chris told us how he had subdued an unruly prisoner, whipping him across the face with a pair of handcuffs. The actor Humphrey Bogart got his lisp from similar treatment at the hands of the Navy Shore Patrol. Casual violence and cruelty were part of the national experience. They weren't limited to obscure prairie towns.

About half a mile west of Marengo on County Highway 212, there was a one-room schoolhouse. An effigy of a man hanging by the neck with a jug in his hand was strung up in a tree there. The thing wasn't very realistic, but it was sinister and frightening. When I asked my dad about it, he said, "Oh, it's supposed to be a bootlegger." I had no idea what that meant, but it was around the time the 18th amendment prohibiting alcoholic drinks was repealed. Bootleggers had made plenty of money out of Prohibition, and it may have been that feelings were running high enough to justify death threats.

Beginning in 1932 or '33, the citizens of Iowa agreed on a packaged liquor law for the state. It limited the sale of hard liquor to state-operated stores where it could be purchased only by the bottle, in a package. It was illegal to have an open bottle of booze in your possession anywhere but in your home. That meant you could not have an open bottle in your car. The idea behind this curious and unenforceable arrangement was that people who drank would find it more convenient to do so in private.

What emerged was a de facto local option, county by county. Whether or not liquor was on sale in any given town pretty much depended on what the local community wanted or would tolerate—as well as on who was being paid off. Some places were very strict, taverns serving only 3.2 % beer, closing at midnight and never open on Sunday. In other towns, you could buy set-ups in any bar with your bottle of whiskey open beside you on the table. Still other places had what were, in fact, nightclubs where mixed drinks of all kinds were served. These establishments were tucked away in remote rural areas. Millersburg, a little town south of Marengo, had a place called "The Flamingo Club" hidden downstairs from a café otherwise entirely devoid of customers. I celebrated my twentieth birthday at the Flamingo Club, after which I was a little reluctant even to think of a twenty-first.

I mention all this because it should be plain enough to anyone who thinks about it that violence and the excessive consumption of alcohol are connected. I started drinking when I went away to the Army, drank steadily for over fifty years and then quit. I've done enough drinking to know what it does to people who let it run away with them. The Saturday-night fights that broke out between young farmers in taverns or dance halls or out in the street always involved one or both of the parties having had one drink too many.

There was an upstairs dance hall in Cedar Rapids where the bouncer was an elderly woman, quite an effective arrangement. She had been a carnival wrestler when she was young, and, while she had a muscle-bound look about her, she could still heave an obstreperous male down the stairs if need be. Wearing long, dark-colored dresses, and her hair knotted up on top of her head, she looked like your best friend's grandma. Nobody wanted it told around that an old gray-haired lady had tossed him out in the street, and the Rainbow Room in Cedar Rapids built up a reputation as a quiet place. Given only a little leeway, however, our well-lubricated boys of summer would happily beat anyone bloody who was foolish enough to stand up in front of them.

— ~

Every August, Marengo held a three-day carnival called Jubilee Days. It was an event that started around 1935. The Depression still had a death grip on the Midwest, so celebrating Jubilee Days was in some ways an act of desperation. Everyone was dead broke, teetering on the edge of disaster, but the men in the Chamber of Commerce gritted their plates and got on with their idea for promoting business. Jubilee Days continued to be celebrated in late August every year from the mid-'30's until the restrictions of World War II shut them down.

A big attraction during Jubilee Days was "The Old Athaletic Show." That's how the barker, King Kong, pronounced it, with the extra syllable for its rhythmic bounce, I suppose. The show's barker was a short, burly man, bald-headed, with a remarkably hairy body, who could produce the most outlandish sounds—a combination of howls and grunts. He didn't have a public address system, but even without one we could hear King Kong all the way from the park to the west end of town—five or six blocks.

The barker was in his late fifties. He always had a young "professional" boxer with him—some kid who knew enough about fighting to stay alive in the ring. The two of them took all comers. The old man dealt with anyone who thought he might like to wrestle, although

I don't remember anyone who ever took him up on it, and the boxer faced those who wanted to put the gloves on.

There was a prize—about five dollars, I think—for anyone who could last three rounds. The pro needed a killer instinct to finish off his opponents in that length of time, but I think it is safe to assume that The Old Athaletic Show never had to shell out any prize money. The boxer had one big advantage. He was sober, while his challengers, goaded on by their pals, were mostly drunk. They were likely to have been the town bullies, which meant the sympathies of the crowd weren't entirely one-sided.

The crowd was warmed up with a little teaser exhibition in front of the tent, but you had to pay to see the real match in the ring inside. Sometimes it got pretty gory. I don't remember anyone beating the pro, and it probably did the bullyboys good to learn that they weren't invincible. Even so, the Old Athaletic Show never completely gratified the lust for battle among the young bulls of the town, and we could look forward to one or two rousing good scraps in the street every night of Jubilee. The best place to watch them was from the Ferris wheel set up in front of the Old Style Tavern.

Domestic violence was so common everyone took it for granted. Only the worst of it was even talked about. Sophie Stevens, one of our neighbors when we lived in Marengo, had a husband who thought it was fun to beat her up. One night her three sons ganged up on their father, got him down, and one of them, Lew, was all set to kill the old man with a poker. Sophie put a stop to it, telling Lew his father wasn't worth going to prison for.

So, my friends, when the evening draws on and people begin to dissolve themselves in nostalgia, don't let anyone start lauding the "good old days," the pre-violence time out in the country when family values, whatever they may be, were strong. Strength, if you could find it at all, lay in a universal determination to keep matters quiet, or to pretend that they just didn't exist.

A Hundred Bushels a Day

Husking corn by hand was the worst job the farm had to offer. I say by hand because before WW II mechanical corn pickers had not yet come into general use. Corn husking season started in October after the first killing frost, and when the corn had begun to dry on the stalk. It was hard, slow work, with the weather worsening as you went deeper into the season. Farmers aimed to get their corn out of the fields before Thanksgiving. After that, the weather in the Midwest could be expected to get seriously bad.

Some women worked in the fields during corn husking, giving a welcome hand with a burdensome job, but I think they also went in order to provide some companionship in a long, grueling and lonely task. Our neighbors, Fern and Everett Timm, worked together husking corn. Fern told me that she and Everett played a game when they picked corn together. Whoever found a red ear—in the days before hybrid seed corn you often came across an ear with all red kernels—was rewarded with a kiss. Fern asked me, with a little glint in her eye, if I thought my folks ever did that. The fact is, my mother never husked any corn, and, even if she had, I think it unlikely she and Aubrey ever played red-ear kissing games.

It takes a good man to pick a hundred bushels of corn a day. The best were urged to enter the yearly corn-husking contests held throughout the state. At the Iowa County corn-husking contest in 1935, prizes for the best huskers were $5, $3 and $2. I guess it was mainly done for the honor of the thing.

On family farms before World War II, the rule was anything that was sold, with the exception of milk and eggs, of course, had to walk off the place. Farmers raised grain to feed to cattle, sheep, and hogs; they didn't sell it to be made into something else like alcohol or a gasoline additive. Manure produced by the livestock went back onto the land, and a cycle of soil replenishment was maintained. All this was long before people started talking about the environment. Still, everyone knew who the "land skinners" were.

Today skinning the land is an accepted way of life, and the land suffers for it. Petroleum-based fertilizers produce yields of over three hundred bushels to the acre, and government policies seem to say 'get big or get out.' Oblivion is the only fate for the kind of farming I knew as a boy.

The corn we intended to feed to livestock was brought in from the field and stored in slatted cribs, not shelled and put into grain bins as it is today. Corn must be dry at the time it is picked if it is to be kept in a crib, otherwise it will get moldy and spoil. Corn shucks retain moisture, so it was important that the corn be picked clean, with no shucks left on the ears. One of the arguments against early mechanical corn pickers was that they picked "dirty," leaving too many shucks to hold moisture and cause spoilage in the crib.

On a nice bright fall day with no wind blowing, the temperature in the '40s and the ground fairly level, corn husking could seem at first to be at least a satisfying occupation. It tended to lose its charm quickly, however, and for any one of a number of reasons. Start with the most common.

It rains a lot in the fall of the year in the Midwest, turning clay fields into quagmires. Few farm wagons had rubber tires in the '30s, and during the war, government restrictions prevented our using them. Instead, we had narrow, iron-tired wagon wheels that sank deep into the mud under a heavy load. Our horses had to work hard just to move a load across a level field. Where it was hilly, as it was on most of the farms in our neighborhood, teams had a particularly tough job, stopping every few steps and holding the wagon in place, so as not to get ahead of the man husking. Believe me, it shifted a farmer's attitude about prayer and the hereafter when his team moved forward several yards, forcing him to bowl the picked ears of corn overhand into his wagon.

Sticky clay mud clung to the husker's feet until they seemed to grow to twice their normal width and weight. Water collected in standing pools where there were low places in the fields, and horses went in halfway to their knees. Then there were the dried stems of smart weeds and morning glories, not to mention Spanish needles and cockleburs, missed in the summer's cultivation, to get tangled around your legs, or to stick matted to your pants.

There were also days when a good, stiff breeze contributed to the fun, when dry corn stalks seemed to dance and dazzle in the bright sunshine making it more difficult to look ahead to spot the next ear of corn to be husked. Stiff leaves on the stalks raked the eyes of the husker. Still, when the weather was dry, it was easier to snap an ear off a cornstalk. Wet weather made the stalks pliant and tough, and you then had to wrestle the ears to get them free of the stalk. An odd point is, with mechanical pickers, it was an advantage to have the corn stalks wet. Machines picked cleaner in wet weather. When it was dry, the loaded wagons were white with unwanted shucks.

Freezing cold eliminated the mud, but it added to the discomfort of work in the field. You can't husk corn wearing heavy clothing. The job calls for freedom of movement in the arms and upper body. We wore our heavy coats when we were driving back and forth from the house to the field, sometimes a matter of a mile or more each way, but once in the field, the warm clothes came off to be hung on the side of the wagon. An extra pair of overalls and a couple of sweatshirts were generally enough for warmth, as long as you kept moving. The discomfort of the cold and a hard-frozen field was better than one ankle-deep in mud.

Downed corn was another thing to contend with. A sleet storm in the fall of the year, or just a heavy rain with a lot of wind, could break the corn down. The routine opening up a field for husking required knocking down one or two rows as the wagons passed over them. On the next round you had to go back and pick up the stalks your wagon had broken down on the first pass. When two huskers worked together on a single wagon, as we did when I went to the field with Aubrey, one of them had to pick up the downed corn behind the wagon. Although this wasn't a job I especially coveted, somehow it often came my way. Sixty years after the event, I can still see the back end of that high-wheeled wagon, the distance between it and me growing steadily greater, and my hopes for salvation getting smaller, as I shucked out my row of downed corn.

Worst of all were the days when it was cold, the temperature just above freezing, and the corn wet from a rain. Then the field was muddy, the stalks were tough and your gloves were immediately soaked through with icy water. I could move fast enough to keep up my body heat, but I never discovered any way to keep my hands warm. Picking corn was a grueling, disagreeable job, one I dreaded as long as I lived on the farm. Getting used to husking corn would be like getting used to suicide.

A yield of a hundred bushels to the acre was a high mark in production to which all farmers aspired before commercial fertilizers, but on most places in the clay hills where we lived, farmers were pleased to settle for a yield of fifty or sixty bushels to the acre. Regardless of whether the yield is good or poor, it takes about the same time for a horse-drawn wagon to inch its way over a field. It may, in fact, take longer where the yield is a poor, because there is a good deal of fumbling involved when you are shucking nubbins off stunted cornstalks.

The number of acres of corn you planted in the spring depended on the manpower you would likely have available at husking time in the fall. Forty acres of corn is only one fifth of the land on a 200-acre farm, and that may not sound like much, but—assuming a yield of a hundred bushels an acre and a man who could husk a hundred bushels a day—it would take well over a month for one man to pick that much corn by hand. With winter coming, you can see why we sometimes picked corn on Sunday.

A man picking corn went to the field with a team of horses and a wagon that held fifty bushels, assuming the ears were heaped up above the top of the box. To make that possible, a set of "bang-boards" was mounted on the wagon on the side opposite the man picking. Inch-thick boards were cleated together in sets of three or four running the length of the wagon. The husker tossed the ears he picked against the bang-boards, and they dropped back into the wagon.

The corncrib on our farm was falling apart when we moved onto the place. It was one of several buildings that had to be rebuilt immediately. We put a new crib up in exactly the same spot where the old crib stood. Although it seemed large to me at the time, our new crib was a smallish structure, built in the conventional way, with cribs on both sides of a driveway, each holding about 2,000 bushels.

People talked about rat-proof corncribs, but I would say that was mostly talk, at least it was where I lived. Even so, we seldom saw a rat.

With all that corn at hand, they were content to stay out of sight while they gorged themselves. It was only when we shelled the corn out of a crib that we disturbed the rats in their nests.

One day when we were shelling corn, we had nearly emptied the crib on the north side by noon when the crew stopped to eat. Only about fifty bushels remained to be shelled. Rats retreated into the small pile, driven there by the noise and the shovels of the crew. When the men came back to work after their noon meal, Aubrey carefully tied the bottoms of his pants legs shut with binder twine. One of the neighbors helping us that day, John Bury, thought the old man's cautious move was pretty funny, and had a good deal to say about it, "Look at that big baby. I believe he's afraid of rats."

As that last fifty bushels of corn disappeared, the place came alive with rats, hundreds of them, and friend Bury had one high inside his pants leg against his thigh. It was a moment when you might have said John was perfectly focused.

Having heard him teasing my dad only a moment before, the crew was interested in how John intended to deal with his problem. He didn't dare let go, but he killed the rat in his hands, in spite of the fact it was clawing his leg raw. After that, everyone went and tied his pants legs shut. Fortunately, the rat turned out not to be rabid, and John Bury lived to tell the story—rather, he lived to listen while it was told about him.

Until rural electrification brought power to the farms around us, there were very few mechanical elevators to ease the task of unloading a wagon full of corn, and those few were found only on the most prosperous farms. The farmers we knew shoveled every ear into the crib by hand, using short-handled number ten scoops at that.

Corn huskers wore cotton-flannel gloves to protect their hands. Husking gloves were made with an extra thumb on the back so that they could be turned over and used again on the other side. When we boys were old enough to husk corn, it was common for us to wear husking gloves to school, a way of showing off how big we were. We let the extra thumb flap, or we pushed it back into the glove if we wanted to look a little more stylish.

Corn huskers wore out one pair of gloves a day. By the time the wagon was full at noon, the working side of the gloves was hanging in shreds and tatters. Then the gloves were turned over (this is where the extra thumb came in), and you wore out the other side during the afternoon. We bought husking gloves in bundles of a dozen pairs each. In 1935, you could get a bundle of Oshkosh b'Gosh gloves at the Trading Post for $1.89.

Some older men talked about husking corn barehanded. There was one brand of corn with deep red-colored and very rough kernels called Bloody Butcher. Old farmers said it was Bloody Butcher when you planted it, and bloody hell when you husked it.

A good team of horses on your wagon made the difference between a hard job and one that was blindingly frustrating. There was no one in the wagon driving the team, and horses were supposed to move forward and to stop on voice command. Lines on the harness were tied off at the front end of the wagon, with the team moving along the row on its own.

On still, frosty mornings in the fall when I was walking to school, I could hear the voices of the men in the field from a long way off talking and swearing at their teams, almost in a chant: Giddap! Whoa! Back! punctuated by the whack of ears landing in the wagon as it crawled along, visible only as a set of bang-boards moving through the standing corn. "Back" was no more than a fond hope. I never saw a team that would back a loaded wagon on its own. It was hard enough to back them when you had hold of the lines.

Huskers wore a peg or a hook strapped over the glove on their right hand to aid them in getting the shucks opened and the ear snapped off the stalk. Grown men all used hooks, while women and kids used pegs.

A peg was a bit of metal three or four inches long and a quarter of an inch wide, bent just a little at one end and made with a blunt point. It was riveted to a leather strap, worn buckled onto the right hand, lying diagonally across the palm with the point up, resting on the forefinger between the first and second knuckle. The point came just under the opposing thumb where it was used to open the shucks on an ear. You had to take care not to throw your peg away when you tossed an ear of corn into the wagon.

Grown men used hooks because they could husk faster with them. Hooks were buckled on around the wrist. They were designed to be worn in the palm of the hand or on the heel of the thumb. Neither one nor the other seemed to give much of an advantage in speed. The choice was a matter of individual preference. Although there were single, double and treble hooks, those fancy hooks were a nuisance because husks and bits of stalk got jammed into them. The fast huskers I knew all used single hooks.

A hook made it possible for the husker to shuck an ear of corn in one unbroken movement: grab, open, squeeze, snap, and throw, all in one smooth, uninterrupted motion—or so Aubrey told me time and again. Toward the end of my time on the farm, I was promoted to the use of a hook, but I never in my life husked a hundred bushels in one day.

This it the way it is supposed to be done. (I can hear the old man's voice as I write out his directions). Grab the ear of corn in your left hand. It works best if the open end of the ear is pointing up, but a good husker can take the ear whether it is pointing up or down. Bring the hook on your right hand hard across the ear tearing the shucks open as you do. With your left hand, squeeze the ear so that it pops out of the shucks. Your right hand grasps the clean ear in passing, snaps it off the stalk and tosses it into the wagon. It is all done in one smooth, unbroken movement.

A good husker looks ahead for his next ear while he is shucking out the ear he has in his hands. The idea is to set up a rhythm for yourself so that you can move quickly, smoothly and without fumbling. A man husking a hundred bushels of corn a day is a blur of action in the field, and he keeps it up hour after hour. If you think any part of that sounds easy, I recommend you try it sometime.

Huskers worked with the wagon on their right side. The team and wagon move along straddling a row already picked, with another picked-out row standing immediately next to the wagon. Working with Aubrey, I had the unpicked row nearer the wagon, while he took the next two rows farther off. In other words, he was picking twice as much as I was. You may judge from what I have already explained that he was moving pretty fast. In order not to break his rhythm, he never looked to see where he was throwing. It requires a real suspension of disbelief to accept that, as long as I didn't duck or flinch, I was safe in the midst of the ears whizzing past me. To do so called for nerves of steel, and mine were never that. I had only to duck reflexively, as I often did, to have the point driven home by a flying ear of Iowa's best, a foot long and rough as a rasp, whanging me on the side of the head.

Corn had to be out of the field and in the crib before Thanksgiving, when the Midwestern winter began to set in hard. You might deal with an inch or two of snow, but a deep snowfall and the drifts that went with it made it impossible for horses and wagons to get through the fields, and then what remained unpicked was lost. There was almost no way to salvage any of it. People driving by fields left in that condition could see at a glance what had happened. Not only was it a financial loss, it was a sure sign of poor farming, and a disgrace to everyone involved. I can tell you it didn't happen at our place.

Husking was especially hard on hands and wrists. I can't claim ever to have done enough of it to have suffered much in that way, but the men who were out in the fields all through husking season developed deep cracks in their fingers and thumbs where the flesh split down to the quick. Their wrists on the hand wearing the hook became swollen and painful from the constant snapping motion. Some men wore leather wristlets buckled on tightly to ease the hurt. In any event, there was no stopping. The advancing season took no account of anybody's pain. Huskers rubbed liniment on their sore wrists, put melted beeswax or Bag Balm in the splits on their fingers, swore a little and kept going.

Good huskers brought in two heaping fifty-bushel loads a day, shoveling the load into the crib as part of the job. They did it day after day until there was no corn left standing in the field, or until bad weather put a stop to all corn picking. When things were tight, picking went on seven days a week, although, even in our non-religious family, it was considered bad luck to work too often on Sundays.

Actually, I don't think religion had much to do with it. It was the fact that seven days a week of that kind of work was more than blood and bone could endure. It is well to remember, too, that the routine work on the farm—milking, feeding stock, cleaning barns and hauling manure—still had to be done along with the major task of getting the corn in.

Aubrey liked to move fast. He worked hard in spurts, and he expected everyone around him to do the same, but he was temperamentally unsuited to a long pull. The day-in and day-out grind of corn husking drove him wild. His mood darkened as the season progressed, and we had at least one domestic uproar before we were finished. The situation was eased only when we had a hired man to help with husking. In a black mood Aubrey had a voice and manner that would change the expression on the face of a Hereford steer, and, even during the Depression when jobs were hard to find, it was quite a trick to keep a man on the place once he had been hired.

When the time came, as it inevitably did, that the hired man got fed up and quit, I sent heartfelt, if furtive, prayers to whatever gods there may have been for some fellow with a strong back and thick skin to turn up at our place looking for work. As Huck Finn discovered when he prayed for a fish line and hooks, there is no reliable return on that kind of supplication. Sometimes it worked; sometimes it didn't.

The mechanical corn pickers they started to use on farms large and small after the war were a mixed blessing. They were tremendous labor savers, but they were probably as dangerous an item as we had to deal with, right up there with unguarded buzz saws. Every year, after farmers started using mechanical pickers, there was news of a man or a boy who had lost fingers, a hand or an arm in a corn-picking accident.

The reason was always the same. They were in a hurry, and hadn't taken time to shut their machines down while they cleared away some stray junk jammed in the snapping rollers, the part of the machine that actually takes the ears off the cornstalks. Why they were in such a hurry when machines had already shortened the time required for picking corn, God alone knew. Maybe they truly believed that time was money. As with a number of the conveniences for farmers in the years following the war, the real price of mechanical corn pickers was high.

Farms were especially dangerous because men so often worked alone, far from help in case of an emergency. I knew one man whose tattered pants cuff got wrapped around an unguarded power take-off shaft on the tractor he was driving. His clothing was old and worn and gave way easily—fortunately for him. The machine tore off every stitch of clothes he was wearing except his shoes, and he went to the house naked but unbroken to get something to cover himself. Owen Thompkins was lucky. A lot of others weren't.

Blizzard

1935

A ubrey and Milt swapped stories about blizzards in Dakota where the land was flat, empty and featureless, where there were no fences; where men and boys got lost in storms, wandering away in the blinding snow, trying to go from the barn to the house; their bodies found months later after the spring thaw. Farmers who wanted to stay alive stretched ropes to guide them from one building to another.

Every farmyard around where we lived was fenced. It wasn't likely that anyone was going to get lost and die in an Iowa storm, not really, but, at the age of eight, my runaway imagination called up an old warrior, with eyes that were dead white when you looked into them. He was Commander of Blizzards, waiting to come down again from the north with all his forces some day when the fences were gone, coming from his place north of the lights we could see in the sky on nights when it was bitter cold.

By mid-afternoon that day late in November 1935, the Iowa sky had begun to get the eerie, flat, gray quality that goes before a heavy snow. It was dark by chore time, and the light from our lantern glowed on occasional flakes of snow beginning to fall softly, steadily increasing in volume as the darkening evening wore on. Milt and I had finished chores, and were on our way to the house, the snow falling thicker, clinging to our eyelashes and blinding us, although there was still no wind.

Milt reached for the lantern I was carrying. "I'll bet you're afraid to do this." He swung the lighted lantern in a circle over his head. "You better not let Aubrey see you do it, though."

Aubrey wouldn't have wanted anybody fooling around with a lighted lantern. The house on our farm burned to the ground only about four years before we moved here, and Aubrey was in the crowd of spectators, and had helped put out a fire that got started in the barn that night. He had a scar on the side of his head where he was hit with a bucket full of water.

"It looks like fireworks when the lantern goes through the snow like that."

Milt squinted up at the falling snow. "Nah. This snow just looks like a swarm of big white flies to me."

Later, when we peered out from inside the house into the pitch black now dappled with falling snow, the beams of yellow lamplight from our kitchen windows revealed a gradually worsening storm. Quietly, as if it were keeping a secret, the wind began to pick up, and the snowflakes became smaller, finer, and harsher, slanting down through the lamplight that streamed out into the night.

The wind continued to rise during supper. Our house, unprotected on its hilltop, shuddered in the heavy gusts, while the gale moaned through the naked limbs of the trees outside. When I heard Aubrey say, "This looks like it might turn into a blizzard," the hairs began to stand up on the back of my neck.

After supper, the men sat in the front room, reading the paper and smoking, listening to the radio. The man who did the news from WHO, Des Moines, was talking about cattle dying on the prairies west of Omaha. Out there, herds had been caught in the open without shelter, and could not be rescued in time to save them. It was cold enough that Maude, who wasn't so great when it came to pets, let my dog come in to sleep in the basement. Normally, she would have said, "That dog can sleep in the barn."

The house shook more as the wind rose still higher. At bedtime, Aubrey went down to the cellar to put some big chunks of slow-burning oak into our furnace, and closed down the drafts so the fire would hold overnight. The furnace kept the house nice and warm downstairs, but it didn't heat my bedroom on the second floor very well. Outside, I could hear the wind shrieking around the house. The ghosts that came with the old white warrior were dancing to their own music.

Maude piled heavy cotton comforters on my bed, and I kept my windows tight shut. We had cotton flannel blankets on our beds instead of sheets. Maude said getting into a bed with regular sheets in the winter was like trying to sleep between two tombstones.

When I woke next morning the wind had dropped, the snow had

stopped falling and everything was still. Sunlight blazed against the ice-coated windows of my room. It was too cold for me to fool around trying to melt a peephole so I could see out. I ran downstairs to dress in the kitchen where it was warm.

Maude was setting the table for breakfast. My mother was thirty-eight years old, but her hair was snow-white. She looked like an actress from the side. Sometimes she talked about how she had wanted to go on the stage. Aubrey always snickered when she talked like that.

"You can't go to school today."

"Why not?"

She opened a door on the side of the range, shook down the ashes, and poked the fire. Then she put in another stick of fuel from the wood box beside the stove. "Well, why don't you look outside, and see for yourself?"

I went to the windows on the east side of the kitchen. They were coated with ice on the inside, the same as the ones in my bedroom, but I pressed my thumb against the ice until I melted a hole I could see through. There was the barn all right, and the buildings in the barn-yard, but from the chicken house under the big oak tree by the road, all the way to the barn, there was nothing but sparkling snowdrifts. The fences and gates behind our house had disappeared. Some tracks showed where Aubrey and Milt had broken through the heavy snow crusts, otherwise the drifts were perfect curves of glittering white. Long, thick icicles hung from the eaves of the house and the barn. Our world had been captured by the armies of the white warrior.

The thermometer on the north side of the house read ten below zero. I was in third grade, and I walked to school, a little less than a mile, crossing the fields and woods north of our house. I was glad Maude said I couldn't go today. It would be hard work, tramping through the drifts. Some places the crusted drifts would have supported my weight, and some wouldn't. That and the cold made walking a whole lot worse.

The back door rattled open and banged shut, and the men went thumping down the steps to the basement where they hung their dirty barn clothes. They were coming in for breakfast. Normally they ate before they went out to do chores, but this morning they did their work at the barn first. It was a sign that Aubrey thought it was too cold to do much outside. They were probably going to stay in by the fire, taking a winter day off.

I looked out the kitchen window again. I could see the steam from the breath of the cattle and horses turned out so they could get some exercise. They couldn't move around in the lot very well. Aubrey and Milt broke open a half a dozen bales of hay to give the stock something to chew on.

Cattle and horses all had to have water to drink at least twice a day, no matter how cold it was, or how much ice froze in the tank.

Our tank heater was a covered iron cylinder set down in the water. We kept a fire burning in it so our cattle and horses could drink. The fire melted the ice a little, and we broke the rest of it up with a mattock. Then we fished out the loose chunks with a manure fork.

White smoke from the stovepipe on the tank heater rose straight up in the still air.

It had a strong, sharp smell of kerosene-soaked corncobs burning. When there was a wind, the falling snow and the smoke swirled and danced together under the eaves of the barn, so mixed up you couldn't tell them apart. I liked to watch storms from the east windows in the kitchen. If the radio was playing while the snow fell, it sometimes looked like the snow and smoke were keeping time to the music.

My mother really needed three skillets to cook breakfast, but she only had one, a big heavy black one, made out of cast iron. First she fried bacon, putting it on a platter in the warming oven over the range when it was done. It was good smoked bacon we had made up for us at the butcher shop in South Amana, not the stuff they called sowbelly, bacon that hadn't been smoked and tasted awful. She used some of the bacon grease to fry a pan full of sliced raw potatoes—she called them fresh fries. I liked the brown parts that stuck around the edges of the pan, but I didn't like the white parts. I put vinegar on fried potatoes when they were white, to give them more flavor. I got teased a lot about that.

The last thing Maude cooked for breakfast was a skillet full of scrambled eggs. She knew a story about a Swede cook who said, "De ekks vasn't gute today, poys, so I scrambled 'em." I think she told that joke about every other day. The eggs were always good at our house. I don't know why she liked that story so much.

Maude tried to time it just right so breakfast was ready when the men came in to eat. That way, nothing would be cold. If breakfast had to wait, she put everything in the warming oven, but then she complained that the food wasn't fit to eat.

Aubrey and Milt came up from the basement wearing clean clothes. They were in their stocking feet. My mother wouldn't let anybody wear barn shoes in the house, only in the basement. Aubrey said, "Where's the coffee?" as soon as he stepped through the door into the kitchen. Aubrey usually felt good in the morning, and he was trying to get a laugh out of Maude. Milt just grinned. He was the hired man, so he didn't say much.

"It's on the stove. Your cups are on the table. Sit down. I'll pour your coffee for you." My mother might laugh at a joke, but she didn't like to kid around when she was busy.

Aubrey rubbed his hands together. They were calloused, and they made a dry, rasping sound, like sandpaper. "My God, it's cold out there."

We sat down at the table in our regular places. Aubrey's chair was next to the outside door; Maude's place was opposite him at the kitchen counter where she could jump up if anybody ran out of food; Milt sat with his back to the windows; I sat across the table from him. The grown-ups had high-backed farm-kitchen chairs. My bench got pushed under the table when I wasn't using it.

Aubrey and Milt were tanned from the sun and the winter wind, but only on the bottom part of their faces. Their foreheads were milk white. Aubrey's face was thin with mean-lines around his mouth. Milt was more reddish looking, and his face was sort of round. He didn't have many lines in his face.

Maude put the food on the table: the platter of bacon, and the scrambled eggs and fried potatoes in big bowls. There was enough for the men to have seconds, if they wanted them, and they always did. There was bread on the table, too, along with butter and jam. The men ate a lot of butter. Maude put it on the table a pound at a time. She'd say, "Easy on the butter, boys, 20 cents a pound." That was another one of her jokes.

Milt looked over in my direction, "How do you get away with staying in here by the stove when we're outside freezing?" Milt and I were friends, but he poked fun at me every chance he got.

"I only have to do chores at night."

"Oh, you only have to do chores at night? I wish I had a deal like that. Aren't you going to school today?"

"Maude says I can't go."

My mother talked over her shoulder without looking at Milt, "When it's ten below, and with these deep drifts, I don't want him out in the wind."

Aubrey was eating his eggs and bacon. He reached for the fried potatoes, "There's no wind now. It's dead still."

He turned to me. "If you want to make up for missing school, you can come out with us this morning, and help clear the road."

My mother chimed in, "He's eight years old, Aubrey. I don't think it will hurt him to stay indoors."

Aubrey finished his potatoes. He pushed his plate back, got out his Bull Durham and papers and started rolling a cigarette.

"All right. Make a sissy out of him then. He can stay in the house until he's ready for high school for all of me."

I ducked my head, and tried to get small enough to disappear. I sneaked a look across the table at Milt. He was busy rolling his own cigarette with his big, thick fingers. It never looked like he was going to get the thin paper wrapped around the loose tobacco, but he always did.

Aubrey finished smoking his cigarette, and put it out in the coffee left in his cup. Maude didn't like it when the men put their cigarettes out that way. She usually said something about it, but Aubrey was already standing up, rubbing the ice away so he could see out the kitchen window. The sky was clear and blue, and the sun made the ice coating on the windows blinding to look at even from inside the house.

"The Bricker boys aren't going to be able to get their truck through here until we clear the road out. One thing about it, the milk won't go sour. It will keep for a week in this cold."

Milt looked up and said, "Yeah, but what are we going to use for milk cans? We've only got a dozen altogether, and three of them are full now."

Aubrey didn't say anything, and Milt went into the front room, where he could see down the road to the west of us. "Looks like Howletts are starting to dig out down there at the end of their lane."

Howletts lived down the hill northwest of us. Bill and Cora Howlett had two kids, a boy, Gene, eighteen years old, and a daughter, Mary, who was fifteen. Everybody in the family was short and fat. When they all got into their car at the same time, the running boards dragged on the road.

Aubrey looked a little bit sore, "If Howletts can clear their lane, we ought to be able to dig the road out wide enough so the milk truck can get through." Howletts didn't have a reputation for being too energetic.

Somebody knocked at the back door. Aubrey went out to the back landing and opened the door and the tarpaper-covered screen door to see who was there. I heard him say, "Come on in, Heinie. We're just finishing breakfast."

It was Henry Eichorn from up the road east of us. He had walked down to our place through the snow. The Eichorns were German, and his proper German name was Heinrich, but everyone except my mother figured Heinie was close enough. Maude rolled her eyes when she heard Aubrey asked Heinie to come in.

Heinie stood in the kitchen doorway, holding the door open, letting the cold in. His wizened-up face and scraggly whiskers peeked out from under a tattered hunting cap. One clear drop hung on the end of his nose. When Heinie wiped it away with the greasy sleeve of his mackinaw, I could see the copper band he wore on one wrist to protect him from rheumatism.

The snow on his feet started melting and ran onto the floor. It was only water, but Maude moved fast, the way she did when she was irritated. She got some newspapers from the front room, and dropped them by Heinie's feet.

"Stand on these papers, Henry—and close the door." Heinie shut the door behind him, and stepped onto the papers, looking uncomfortable.

"Do you want some coffee?" The tone of Maude's voice said drink it and go.

His answer was a whine, "Ach, Gott, ja, dot vould be gudt."

"Dick, let him have your bench."

I got up, pushed my bench over to Heinie, and then bent down on the register to lace on my high-top boots. They had been standing on the register to keep them warm. I made sure they were always clean so Maude would let me wear them in the house. Heinie sat down to drink his coffee. He looked over his cup at my mother and very carefully asked, "You haff, maybe, a liddle suchar?"

Maude's voice was colder than the outdoors, "There's sugar on the table, Henry. Help yourself."

Heinie slurped his coffee, and started talking to Aubrey. "Ve ver tinking, maybe, ve coudt all get togetter und clean out dese rotes today yet. Undt my poyss coudt gif a handt mit."

It was generous of Heinie to offer himself and his two boys to help clear the roads, especially when he didn't have a car. He must have been planning—Maude looked like she had already guessed it—to ask us for a ride into town.

Maude turned to me, "Dick, you dress yourself warm if you're going outside to help."

You could never be sure what Maude would do next. Aubrey looked up like he was surprised at this switch around, but he didn't say anything. Maude was probably trying to get all of us out of the house, so she could clean up the kitchen.

She said to me, "You can take that shovel I keep by the furnace." My mother had a small scoop she used to clean out ashes. "And don't forget to put it back when you're finished." She was always afraid her tools would wander away and get mixed up with the farm clutter.

I went down to the basement to get ready to go outside. I had on a flannel shirt, jeans stuffed into my boots and a thick sweater over my shirt. A pair of overalls went on top of everything I was already wearing. Then came my outside clothes: lumberman's rubbers over my boots, a sheep-lined mackinaw and a cap with earflaps and mittens. The mittens were the part that didn't work so well. My hands always got cold first, and there didn't seem to be anything I could do to keep them warm.

Aubrey and Milt wore horsehide mittens with separate knitted wool liners, but those things were too big for me. Aubrey took a look at me while he finished dressing. "Now that you've got all that stuff on, how are you going to move?" That was his favorite kind of joke.

Except in the bitterest weather, he wore a couple of sweatshirts and a second pair of overalls when he worked outside, and that was all. He said the only way to keep warm was to move fast. That was all right for him. He knew what he was going to do next, but I had to stand around freezing, waiting for him to tell me what he wanted me to do.

We trooped out the back door. My heavy clothes made my arms stick out like a stuffed doll. The cold clamped down on my face so hard I could hardly take a breath through my nose, and breathing through my mouth made my teeth ache.

I took Maude's shovel and walked out to where the snow had drifted over our front gate. The drift was level with the top of our mailbox. Aubrey and Milt went to the corncrib to get their shovels, number ten scoops they used for ear corn. With short handles they weren't the best things for shoveling snow, but that's all anyone had to work with.

At the top of the hill in front of our house, the road was level for a few dozen yards. Along there the wind had scoured the road clean, but where the hills dropped off to the east and west of us, the high banks along the road caught the blowing snow, and then places between the banks drifted level full. The rose bushes, flowering plums, and pussy willows that grew on the banks and were so pretty in spring and summer, made the snow drift deeper there in winter, anywhere from a foot to six feet deep, crusted over hard enough to support a man's weight.

Heinie was standing in the middle of the road looking back toward his farm, waving his arms in the air. I thought he was just acting crazy, but then I could see two people starting out from his house, walking toward our place. It was his two boys—the older one, also called Heinie—and the younger one, about my age, whose name was Harold, but everybody called Pete.

Bill and Gene Howlett were working their way up the road toward us from the west, and it looked as if the three Hartzes from farther down the road had joined them: Big Jim, Little Jim—a year older than me—and Maury, Little Jim's older brother who was almost a grown man.

We were coming together along the road like minutemen called out to fight a foreign enemy, only these soldiers weren't Redcoats like in the stories about Paul Revere. The snow was our enemy. We were hastily armed farmers standing in the path of a white-uniformed force determined to bury us, to cut us off from our supplies, to starve us into submission. We were a platoon left behind to fight a hopeless fight against the white invader. We would stand our ground and die on the spot if we had to.

We started digging in front of our mailbox. Somebody measured off what they thought was wide enough for a car. Aubrey kept arguing that we had to make it wide enough to let Bricker's milk truck get through. The snow broke out in chunks instead of in shovels full. You had to cut a block away from the drift, and then try to throw it off to one side. Most of the time, that meant picking up the block of snow in your hands, and giving it a toss. I was too small to be much use at that kind of work, but I whittled away at a kind of trench I made along-side Milt. Aubrey, with Heinie and his boys, were working a few yards ahead of us. Eventually we all came together; that strip of road was cleared and we went on to the next drifts.

The grown men looked like they were thinking about how their backs ached, and how cold their hands and feet were, but they couldn't say so, and they sure couldn't go inside to warm up. Anybody who did that might as well have published in the paper that he was a weakling and a wimp.

"Did you hear about him? Went to the house with the kids to warm up. Can you beat that? Like to have him around when things get tough?"

By the time we got to the bottom of the hill west of our house, the cold was eating into my hands and feet. The hickory handle of my shovel felt like an icicle through my mittens. Jimmie Hartz was swinging his arms, flapping them around his body, trying to warm up his hands. Milt had his eye on us, and he said, with his voice down a little bit, "Why don't the two of you go back to the house and get warm?" Aubrey was working down the road from us, so I didn't think I had to ask him if I could go.

We stumbled to the house on our half-frozen feet, and I asked Jimmie, "What do you say we take our sleds over to the big hill when we get the road finished? When the road's dug out, it should be good sliding."

"Nah. Everybody's going to go to town this afternoon."

He was right about that. I hadn't thought of it. "Well, what about tomorrow? It's Saturday."

"Yeah, well, I'll think about it."

I don't know what it was about Jimmie Hartz. He never seemed to want to do anything I wanted to do. It made me feel bad, and I gave up. We were too cold to talk, anyway.

We peeled off a layer or two of clothes in the kitchen, and sat in front of the range with our feet on the open oven door. Maude put our mittens up on the warming oven to dry. Both of us had chill blains. Our feet hurt and itched furiously when they began to warm up. Maude made us take our socks off and put our feet in basins of cool water. That helped some.

After our feet stopped hurting so much, we got dressed all over again and went back outside to dig. When Aubrey saw us coming back, he laughed and yelled, "Too cold for you boys?" Jimmie went back to work beside his brother. Milt waved to me, "You come over here and give me a hand."

By two o'clock, we had fought our way out, making a break-through, cutting a narrow lane in the drifts all the way over to the state highway a mile east of our farm. Our little cluster of farms was freed from snow prison for a moment, at least: Eichorn's, to the east a quarter mile; Howlett's, down the hill west of us; and Hartz's, a quarter of a mile farther west. Then everybody went home as fast as they could to get their cars, and go to town for groceries and the mail. Their backs may have ached, but the road was open. We had defeated the old white warrior and his men.

Maude looked pretty sour when Heinie asked if he could ride to town with us, but Aubrey said, "Oh, sure, plenty of room."

We had a Ford V-8 with a front and a back seat, but only two doors, and it was jammed with five people. I was squeezed between Milt and Heinie on the back seat, my feet on the hump in the floor over the drive shaft. With so many people in the car, the windows fogged over right away. There wasn't any heater or a defroster, so we had to keep the windows rolled down a little bit, cold or not. A lot of the drifts were too high to see over from inside the car. In some places we scraped on both sides between snow banks where we hadn't made the lane wide enough. It was a pretty sure thing that Harv and Marv Bricker wouldn't get their truck through unless they did some digging on their own, but they always carried shovels and chains with them. They knew all about how our roads got in bad weather.

Marengo was crowded with farmers who had dug themselves out, hurrying to buy groceries, trying to get home before it started to snow again. The town's plows had pushed snow up in big piles all around the square. Kids were playing king of the hill up and down the snow ridges. It looked like they had turned the whole park into one big snow fort.

When we started home everybody in the car except Aubrey, who was driving, was holding sacks of groceries. He was the only one who could see out. The rest of us were buried under stuff we had bought. We had our supplies now, and we could hold out for a long time. It was a good thing too, because the bright morning sunshine was gone. Overhead now was another gray snow-sky. During the early afternoon, the temperature got up to somewhere around zero, but it was beginning to fall again.

It was bitter cold and dark by the time we started evening chores. Off to the north, the sky glowed a dull, sullen kind of glow. The old warrior was getting his armies ready for another try at us.

We were just about finished with supper and the men were all set to go in the front room and listen to the radio, when the telephone rang for our farm—two long rings and two shorts. We could tell it was from a neighbor, because the ring was kind of feeble and weak instead of the strong ring it had when the call came from Central in town.

Maude was the only one who answered the phone at our house. I heard her say, "Thanks for letting us know, Jim." Maude came back into the kitchen. Her face was blank, like she was thinking. "Aubrey, that was Jim Hartz. He said we should turn on WHO, Des Moines. They're talking about a bad storm coming tonight. They say this one looks like it might be a real, old-fashioned blizzard."

Hotel Doose

I was a senior in Marengo High School, sixteen years old, in 1943–'44, staying with my grandparents in town Sunday night to Friday, and suffering out the weekends on the farm. Everything about high school was easy for me, and I loved it, except for the fact I was always broke. My allowance was fifty cents a week. Even when the picture show cost ten cents, soft drinks were a nickel and admission to the weekly dances upstairs at the old opera house was a quarter, half a dollar didn't go all that far. I heard my grandpa say that Gilchrists, who ran the Doose Hotel, were looking for a student to work as a night clerk, and I went over, not feeling any too keen about it, to apply for the job.

The Doose Hotel—I never heard anybody call it the Hotel Doose, but that's what it said on the front window—was a two-story building across the street from the town square. The hotel entrance was two doors north of the corner. The door to the hotel's dining room was next, and Emma Graber's millinery shop was north of that.

Mrs. Gilchrist had only recently stopped serving meals on a regular basis in the dining room, probably because of the war, food shortages and difficulties in getting help, but she kept the room set up, the tables complete with place settings, cloths, silver, glassware and all, and she served meals on rare occasions—for the Chamber of Commerce meetings or for weddings. The place was kept sparkling clean. It was decorated like most old-fashioned country hotels with potted palms and such.

As the war dragged on, however, it was clear that Mrs. Gil, and the one or two women she was able to hire, couldn't handle the extra load of the hotel dining room, and the dining room area was converted into a tavern. It was still a tavern after the war when Gilchrist sold the hotel, and he and his wife retired from business altogether.

Over the way in the park across from the hotel, there was a merry-go-round Mr. and Mrs. Gilchrist had donated to the kids in town.

In summer, the Gilchrists put wooden lawn furniture on the sidewalk in front of their hotel for themselves and their guests to enjoy the cool evenings outside, where they could see what was going on in the park—the Saturday night band concerts, kids playing on the merry-go-round, that sort of thing.

Although Gil was a great friend of my grandpa, I knew him and his wife only on sight. Everyone I knew spoke of Gil as a real gentleman, but most agreed his wife was harder to get to know. I'd heard that she was kind of an ogre. My information about Mrs. Gilchrist came mainly from the three youngest kids in the Thomas family, my cousins, all of whom had worked for her at one time or another. To hear them tell it, she was crabby, mean, a tyrant, stingy and a bad cook. Later, after I had worked for her for a while, I found she was almost exactly the opposite on all counts. I never understood my cousins' bad feelings toward her, although it is true she was hard to get to know at first.

Mrs. Gilchrist was a little woman, very formal in manner, who spoke rather slowly in a soft voice. Even though she was heavily wrinkled, her dark auburn hair was always neatly done up, not a hair out of place. Her glasses were pince-nez on a retractable chain she wore pinned to her dress. The pinch-on glasses made deep grooves in the sides of her nose. Some years earlier, before she and Gil were married, she had been in an automobile accident and was thrown out of an open car. Her hip was broken, and for some reason the break never healed properly. Mrs. G. used one crutch when she walked. Everyone who worked at the hotel was warned about spilling anything where she might put her crutch in it and slip. I never heard her complain, but it may have been pain from her hip that gave her a pinched look.

Mrs. Gilchrist explained the duties of the night clerk to me. I was to attend to the front desk, to help guests in with their luggage, get them registered, sell them stamps if those were needed and generally make everyone welcome. Once a week, I was to wash the big front windows that looked out on the street from the lobby, and, in winter, I was to keep the sidewalk in front cleared of snow. It was light work, and my wages were accordingly light—a dollar a night, plus my evening meal and any tips I might get. The going tip was ten cents a bag, occasionally as much as a quarter, or very rarely fifty cents—from some big spender. Gil showed me the bell-hop's trick of carrying four bags at one time—a big one in each hand, and a smaller one tucked under each arm. He winked and said it was a way to get a bigger tip.

It was clear that working as the hotel night clerk was going to be easy enough, but it took away all my leisure time after school, from four in the afternoon until midnight. Leaving my pals and going off to work every day right after classes didn't have much appeal. I was caught in a silly dilemma. I now had as much spending money as I needed, but I didn't have any time free to spend it.

I felt pretty sorry for myself at first, but then my friends began to drop around to visit, and things didn't seem so bad. Mrs. Gilchrist didn't approve of most of my buddies, especially the girls. She called them chippies. I didn't know what that meant until I looked it up, and then I never bothered explaining it to the girls. I had to restrict my social life to Saturday night, but the change jingling in my pocket took the sting out of my new restrictions.

Guests at the Doose Hotel were almost all traveling salesmen. Most of them had had the same territories for years, and they were thoroughly acquainted with the Doose, which was a good thing, because the place had some odd features. There were about fifteen rooms altogether, all but two of them on the second floor. Only one room, the bridal suite, if you please, had a lock and a key. Doors to the other rooms could be fastened from the inside, but they could not be locked when the occupant went out. Try explaining that to some traveler from Chicago or points east making his way through the wilds of the Midwest for the first time, especially when you, the explainer, are a spindly, callow-looking sixteen-year-old.

Another feature of our hotel that got greenhorns excited was the fire escape, or rather, the lack of fire escapes. To be sure, the building was only two stories high, but there were no ladders or outside stairs leading to the street. Under the windowsill in the second-story rooms there was a coil of manila rope with knots in it every eighteen inches. The rope was tied into a metal ring in the floor. I know now that only a person in excellent physical condition could have used a thing like that to get to the street, but I accepted it as I did anything else where adults were concerned. It was the way things were, and that was all there was to that.

Three of our rooms had baths. A room with bath rented for two dollars and fifty cents a night. The bridal suite went for three dollars, but it didn't have a bath. I guess the married couple was supposed to have washed up before they arrived. That room was almost never used, partly because Mrs. Gil liked to save it for the people who ran the Old Style Tavern. They closed late, around midnight, and they had a long drive to their home outside of town. In winter especially, when the weather was bad and they preferred not to risk the roads, Mrs. G. had me put them in the bridal suite. The wife hated it, and complained to me about it behind her hand, "It's so big, and all that dark furniture." I tried to convey the lady's misgivings to my boss without hurting her feelings, but I never had any luck at it.

Rooms without bath rented for a dollar and a half a night. There was a clean bathroom down the hall. The hotel wasn't dirty, it was just plain. We also had three inside rooms with no windows that cost only fifty cents a night. Mary Howlett, the chubby neighbor who saw me safely to school my first year on the farm, lived in one of the inside rooms. Mary did scullery work at the hotel, and it is just possible she did a little something more on her own in the way of entertaining. I can't say for certain.

We had some characters around town for whom Mrs. G. felt an inside room was plenty good enough. She gave me thorough instructions on how to spot a drunk coming across the park. "You don't want the ones who stagger, but you don't want the ones who walk too straight, either." They had to be kept out because of the likelihood they'd vomit and make a mess. I got to be fairly good at it, and we had no drunks at the Doose Hotel during my tenure as night clerk.

There were nights we had only one or two guests registered, when boredom was my worst enemy. After I had read the evening paper, I was free to use the big table in the lobby to do any homework I might have, but I was supposed to wait until the salesmen were finished with their paper work. There was a small radio at the desk that was turned off when Mr. and Mrs. Gilchrist went to bed. I read, or I listened to the clock in the lobby. It had a second hand that clicked when it moved. I never got used to that click.

Doose, the name of the hotel that was a puzzle to me when I first went to work there, turned out to be the name of a German who originally owned the place. One of the relics of the first owner's time was an oak card table with shelves built into each corner to hold beer steins. That table survives today, although how it has been kept out of the hands of antique hunters I can't say. It is still part of the hotel furniture, all that remains of the Doose Hotel lobby as I knew it.

I ate my evening meal in the unused dining room. My table was set near a connecting door so I could keep my eye on the front desk while I was eating. Mrs. Gilchrist prepared my suppers in the hotel's big, dark old kitchen. Using a crutch as she did, Mrs. Gilchrist could not carry anything heavy, and I would be called from the lobby to pick up my meal on a tray.

Her food was tasty even though it was mainly the meat and potatoes diet of the Midwest. She almost always served soup as a starter, and she sometimes had bleu cheese and crackers for dessert. That was about as different as it got, but it was out of the ordinary for me and I must say I enjoyed it. I have a feeling that it may have been the slight unfamiliarity of Mrs. G's meals that was behind my cousins' complaints about her cooking. I knew they often had nothing to eat but bread, but the conservatism bred of poverty is hard to shift. Faced with her soup and blue cheese, they were prepared to go down swinging for their bread, like farmers who had their land sold out from under them, but stayed Republican until the day they died.

Mr. Gilchrist was an aristocratic-looking gentleman with straight white hair and a Roman nose. His first name was Roland, although I never heard him called anything but Gil. He was a life-long Democrat. A big picture of an extremely youthful Franklin D. Roosevelt hung in the hotel lobby. For his faithful services to the party, Gil held an appointment as Marengo's Post Master—a kind of general manager at the post office—all through the Roosevelt Administration.

He wasn't in any way puffed up or arrogant, but Gil had a proper sense of himself, and he dressed accordingly. Turned out in a dark suit and a snow-white shirt—never a colored shirt—he looked ready to step off on parade. He habitually wore a black bow tie, and he never went out on the street without a hat. In summer, that meant a Panama or a sailor straw, and, in winter, a pearl-gray Homburg. When the weather was cold, he wore spats, but I never saw him wear a topcoat. Mrs. G. used to fuss at him a lot about that, just as my wife does with me when she thinks I'm going out improperly dressed for the cold.

Gil and I had an evening ritual that never varied. He arrived at the hotel from the post office a little after five while I was eating my supper in the dining room. Every night Gil came through the door from the lobby with the same question, "Well sir, have you been a pretty good boy today?" Please notice, it was not plain "good," but "pretty good." Gil was a realist. I assured him I had been just that. "All right then," and he put a quarter on the corner of the table. He never failed. Then he was on his way to eat his supper with Mrs. G. in the gloomy hotel kitchen.

Mrs. Gilchrist was a widow with two daughters when she met and married Gil. I think she may have been a few years older than her new husband. She seemed ancient to me, but my mother said she remembered Mrs. G. as quite an elegant-looking lady. Probably, it was to preserve that opinion in the world that she wore a wig.

I had heard about the wig from my cousins, but the report was confirmed for me one night when I had to ask for the cash box after Mr. and Mrs. Gil had gone to bed. They kept a room for themselves across the hall just off the lobby, because Mrs. G. couldn't manage steps with her crutch. We had no safe at the hotel, so they took the cash box and stamps into their room when they turned in for the night.

Although it was late, a guest had insisted on buying stamps, and when I knocked and was admitted to their room, there was the wig on a form on the dresser, and Mrs. Gilchrist in bed wearing a mob-cap over her white fringe. I liked Mrs. G. in spite of my cousins' complaints about her. She was strict about what she wanted, and how she wanted it done, but she was fair, and I was afraid I might have done something to embarrass her. Evidently my fears were for nothing; not a word was ever said about the incident. From then on, however, I checked the placement of the wig on the sly, to see if there was any day-to-day variation in the way she wore it. If there was, I never spotted it.

After supper, Gil read his paper in the lobby, and talked with his guests, most of them old friends. He had had a fairly adventurous life when it was all added up. Tucked away under that gentlemanly exterior he had the voice and manner of a slimmed-down Sidney Greenstreet, the fat villain in *The Maltese Falcon*.

Gil told me how, as a young man, he had trained to be a dentist, but had given it up because he disliked the work, I think probably because of the pain he would have had to inflict on his patients. At the time he was fixing teeth, dentists used slow-turning drills powered by foot treadles. You needed the moral fiber of a Plains Indian to go to the dentist in those days.

As a very young man in search of adventure, Gil had tried to enlist in the Army for what would then have been the last gasp of the Indian wars in the West. News of the massacre at Wounded Knee (at that time it was called the Battle of Wounded Knee) balked his career as a soldier, I'm happy to say. He went to Fort Riley in Kansas to join up, and he was there long enough to get to know a veteran sergeant. Gil liked to tell how he teased the leathery NCO, asking him what he would do if they were to get into a fight with the Indians. The old soldier seemed taken aback for a moment, but then replied, imperturbably, "Why, I'd do just what the Captain told me."

The great adventure of Gil's life, a story he told over and over to his guests, was shipping as a stoker on a freighter bound for Bremerhaven. Fuel for the coal-burning furnaces had to be laid in precisely according to a pre-set pattern, each shovel-full exactly in its required spot in order to produce maximum heat. Furnace doors could not be left standing open while the fire was being fed, but had to be closed after every shovel-full was tossed in. They used the loaded shovel to reopen the doors for the next toss. Stokers flipped their shovels up in front of their faces to protect themselves from the fierce heat. Even so, Gil said his face was scorched bright red on all the high points: chin, nose, cheeks and forehead.

When the officers on his ship found Gil better educated than the rest of the black gang, and that he was capable of lively, intelligent conversation, they often invited him to eat with them. That got him into a lot of trouble with his shipmates who were sure he was a spy for the brass. He said he was in a fight every day of the voyage.

At Bremerhaven, the crew found Buffalo Bill's Wild West Show in town, performing on a European tour. The ticket-seller wanted to know where the boys were from when they showed up at his booth. They told him the United States was home, and he waved them in to see the show free of charge.

Gil often talked about the Red scare that hit the States after the First World War. He thought it was nonsense, and he made no secret of his scorn for people who were afraid of the "Bolshevikis." He said he had never seen a Bolsheviki, and wouldn't have known what to do with the critter if one had presented itself.

One night when I was alone in the lobby, our town marshal, Carl Seckel, brought in an old man so drunk he could barely walk. Barney Baughman was a dwarfish little fellow who made his living taking care of yards and doing odd jobs around town. Because of Mrs. Gilchrist's rules, I didn't want to put him up at all, but Carl insisted on it, and he was the authority. We got Barney into an inside room, and although he was ready to pass out, we managed to get him out of his clothes and into bed. I had never seen a man naked outside of my own family, and I was struck with how pathetic the old fellow looked with his clothes off.

We had just got him covered up in bed, when I heard Carl making clucking noises of disapproval. "My God, look at this." Barney was carrying $2,200 in cash. It was the winter of 1943, so I suppose the money must have been worth at least ten times that amount now. Earlier that same day, Barney had drawn all his life's savings out of the bank, and had gone on a spree in a tavern across the park buying drinks for everyone in sight. We had deadbeats enough around town who were more than willing to drink up the old man's cash, but somebody at the tavern had had the good sense to call the marshal, and have poor Barney picked up. Carl insisted that I count the bills I suppose in order to have a witness in case questions were asked later, but nothing more came of it. Barney's money went safely back into the bank, and the old fellow himself went back to his work mowing lawns.

Chronic bronchitis bothered me more than usual that winter. Some nights I must have kept all the guests in the hotel awake with my barking until the stroke of midnight when my tour finished, and I could make my way across our dead-quiet town to my grandparents' home. The cough got so bad that in desperation I resorted to an old wife's remedy, and a risky one, of a few drops of kerosene on a little sugar. You hold it in your mouth until the sugar melts. God knows what the result might have been if I had choked and sucked some of that petroleum-based mixture down my windpipe.

It was also during that winter I came down with scarlet fever, my last go-round with the childhood diseases. A year or two earlier, I had been quarantined in town, first for mumps, later for chicken pox, and then, still later, on the farm, for measles. Fortunately for my poor grandma, for whom one trip a day up and down the steep stairs in her house was quite enough, I got the unmistakable symptoms of scarlet—vomiting and a high fever—on a Friday night after I had returned to the farm for the weekend. That was one time when we did call the doctor. Scarlet fever was a serious business. You might come out of it with damage to major organs—heart, liver, kidneys—sometimes weakened eyesight.

Campbell Watts, Dr. Watts' son, also a physician, came out to the farm, and put me in quarantine for three weeks. It was like being sentenced to solitary confinement. There was no television, of course, I wasn't allowed to read, and daytime radio programs didn't have much appeal for me. I put in three excruciatingly dull weeks in my room upstairs at the farm.

While I was quarantined, Aubrey passed my room twice a day for twenty-one days. During that time he never once spoke to me, never said good morning, not once asked how I felt. It was as if I were not in the house. Now, the truly bizarre part of all this was that I didn't notice it. It was a matter of course, nothing out of the ordinary. It was years later when thinking about it, I realized how strange it had been.

The Gilchrists bore with me during my illness, holding my job open for me, substituting one of my cousins from the Thomas family. I continued as night clerk at the Doose Hotel right up until I graduated. The slight scholastic demands I encountered in high school gave me a taste for what I thought would be the frivolities of student life. I was determined to go on to college.

Aubrey had made it clear to me that when I graduated from high school his responsibility for my education was over. His plan was for me to work for him on the farm. He didn't say anything about wages. I was rescued by the Army's having a school program for seventeen-year-olds who were willing to enlist. I grabbed it, and found myself on my way to a college engineering program for which I was absolutely unprepared. I had just turned seventeen.

The Rock Island Railroad and its Rockets are both gone now.

Only the unused tracks lie there as a reminder. I went away too, just a little ahead of the Rock Island, in May 1944 when I took one of the new Rockets out of Marengo to Des Moines, reporting at Camp Dodge on my way to the Army and to a different life.

After a disastrous summer at Kansas State College in Manhattan trying hard, but unsuccessfully, to get a grip on engineering, I found myself in a group selected for transfer to Japanese Area and Language Studies at Yale University—exactly what I had wanted from the start. I had just about recovered from that thrill when the time came for a furlough.

A first homecoming is like no other. At four in the morning, I stepped off the train at the coal chutes east of town, where the Rock Island from Chicago made its regular, unscheduled, stop. I had been away for six months, and I was astonished to see that nothing had changed during my absence. The town was dead still, empty as a stage setting, as I trudged along the snowy streets to my grandparents' house.

The front door was locked. I got in by crawling through the dining room window next to Mom's sewing machine. The un-oiled wheels squealed when I pushed it aside. I knew that Mom wasn't going to hear anything this side of the Last Trump, but Pop was a light sleeper. The noise woke him, and he was downstairs in his nightshirt to greet me before I could get out of my overcoat. The lights in the hall woke Mom. My uniform was saturated with cigar smoke after the long train ride, and the first thing Mom said to me was, "You've been smoking!" It wasn't true; I hadn't yet started to smoke, but at seventeen the accusation alone made me feel like a man.

After I returned home that Thanksgiving in 1944, I realized I had stepped over a dividing line, and that my life on the farm was over.

The author (*l.*)with Maude, Aubrey and Morey, c. 1944–45

The Big Hill

When we looked out the kitchen windows of our house on the farm, we saw a big hill standing like a wall about a half a mile east of us. The road went up and over the crest of the hill, but our view was cut off entirely in that direction. When cars roared by our house trailing their enormous coils of yellow clay dust, we saw the last of them dropping out of sight over the big hill. That was the end of them. They might just as well have fallen off the edge of the earth.

No matter how hot the weather, no matter how oppressive it was anywhere else, there was always a cool breeze at the top of the big hill. As a kid, I used to go to sit in the shade of the two oak trees there, and to try to puzzle out my life. When that didn't get me anywhere, I stayed to enjoy the shady breeze and the view out over the Iowa River valley, while I let slide what I couldn't understand.

From the hilltop I could see almost four miles northwest toward town—where I wanted to be. At that distance, the town looked like a mat of treetops, something painted by Grant Wood. Three spikes broke through the trees to show that there was a town there at all: the water tower near the depot with MARENGO painted on it in big black letters, the red tiles of the court house tower and the black spire of the Catholic church topped with a white cross.

Across the timber in the river valley north of where I was sitting, farmhouses and barns looked like toys, tiny dots of color. Occasionally a flash of sunlight glanced off the windshield of a car so far away you really couldn't see it. Hawks floated in slow circles over the fields on the near side of the Iowa River. The steam trains I could see away down in the trees along the river, blew white steam—the color of death—as they whistled and wailed, mourning things soon be lost.

The hill where I sat enjoying the shady breeze we called the "Eighty Hill," because it was part of an eighty-acre piece of land Aunt Mary brought as her dowry when she married Tom Willis, Aubrey's uncle. They had owned the farm where we moved in the early '30s.

Not many years in the past, the entire hill where I sat had been wooded, but by the time we moved to the farm in 1933, the trees had almost all been cut down, and the hill was covered with stumps. We broke them off, or pulled them out of the ground and used them for firewood.

On the east side of the hill the pasture was all pocked from some-one using dynamite to blast stumps out. My pals and I pretended those scooped-out places were rifle pits. We used them to fight off Indian attacks or to defend our lines against Civil War rebels. Later, as we learned about the war in Europe, we called them foxholes. Only two oak trees were left at the top of the hill, lonely reminders of the thick stand of timber that had once grown in what was now pasture.

Old farmers in the neighborhood told me about an Indian trail that was supposed to have run somewhere near the bottom of the hill—no one knew exactly where. A short distance beyond the toe of the ridge, however, there were three mounds, one large and two smaller. People said they were Indian burial mounds. We didn't know anything more about them than that, so I made up an explanation for myself: the big mound was the grave of a chief, and the two smaller mounds held the bodies of his squaws.

Aubrey talked about digging into the mounds to see if we could find any stone relics, but he never got around to doing it. While we often picked up arrowheads and spear points in our fields, the graves that might have contained more of the same kind of thing remained undisturbed. Later, when the fence was moved over to include the mounds as part of the cornfield, the three hillocks gradually disap-peared under cultivation. It was sad in a way, and yet maybe it was right for the last traces of those ancient people to vanish like that, melting back into the earth they thought of as their mother.

Before our roads were graded, the road over our big hill seemed wickedly steep. All the rest of our road was sticky clay, but that stretch over the hill was sandy. No one ever got stuck there. Wet sand isn't hard to drive a car through, so the steepest hill on our road was also the least troublesome. Later, when roads all over the county were graded, the sides of the banks were sliced down, the top of the hill was scraped away and the approaches to its top were filled in.

It may have had something to do with the fact of the Indian burial mounds, or maybe because I often went to the hilltop to mull over my concerns, that the big hill came to have a kind of religious aura for me, although I never told anyone about that. After Aubrey died in 1975, I had what I suppose might properly be called a vision related to that place. I wasn't asleep, so I can't say it was a dream, but suddenly, for no reason, I saw myself as a small boy sitting on the grass with Aubrey in the shade of the trees at the top of the big hill. He appeared to be quite young, twenty-five or thirty at most. He was strikingly handsome, dressed all in white.

We were looking north from the top of the hill, out over the Iowa River valley, and he was telling me what a beautiful place it was. He made a broad gesture with his arm taking in the entire valley below us, as if he were making me a present of everything we could see. That was all there was to it, nothing more.

Recently I'd been thinking that when the time came for me to die, I'd like to have what is left of me taken back to the farm. I got in touch with the people who now own the place where I grew up, and got their permission for my ashes to be scattered under the trees at the top of the big hill east of the house. I discussed my idea with their neighbor, the man who now actually farms our old place, and he endorsed it. "It's right that you should come back here to where you started."

I thought I had it all satisfactorily worked out, but then, about a year later, there was a terrible storm in the fall of the year. Timberlands all along the Iowa River were devastated. Trees were blown over in such numbers it looked as if a giant hand had pushed them down flat. The worst of the damage was in the valley close to the river, but, even as far away as our farm, trees went down, including one of the two that had survived for so many years at the top of the big hill. When I first saw what had happened, I felt as if I had lost an old friend.

It was silly, I suppose, for me to have assumed that those two trees would be there forever, but now that one of them is gone, I'm no longer so sure I want that hilltop to be my final resting place after all. Why the absence of one tree should make so much difference to me, I really can't say. Maybe I just don't want to die, and I'm looking for an excuse to get out of it.

Last Act and Final Curtain

When I started this account of the farm and Marengo and the things I could remember from when I was a boy, I had it in mind to revisit—at least in my imagination—the places I knew when I was young, in effect, to see all my old friends once more. Now, having written it, I realize, like Emily in *Our Town*, that going home is not a good thing to do. Oh, it is possible to go back, all right, never mind that so many say you can't.

The trouble comes from the double-exposure effect you get when you look at the places you remember, seeing them as they are now and, at the same time, as they were then, both changed and unchanged. That is true for people you once knew. They see you, and remember you in the same way, and you watch them doing it.

Pop and I had a ritual we developed over the years. As a little kid, I got into the habit of saying, "So long, Pop," whenever we parted, and he always answered me the same way. The family, especially my grandma, grinned about it.

When I came home from graduate school at Northwestern in the summer of 1950, Pop was in bad shape. He had lost a lot of weight and he was the color of old ivory. His ears looked longer now that his face was so gaunt. We didn't talk about it, but I could see he was dying. He knew it, too, but sickness didn't take his nerve. Practicing pagan that he was, Pop told the Lutheran minister who came to visit him, "If everybody behaved as well as the Masons, we'd be living in a better place."

When the time came for me to go back to school and I went to say, "So long, Pop," his answer was different, "Goodbye, Dickie." He knew—both of us knew—that we would never see each other again. I lost my nerve, turned away so he wouldn't see me cry and ran to the waiting car.

Pop died in 1950 just before Halloween. He had been a big man, but age and illness shrunk him and none of his clothes fit. He was buried in the suit I wore for high school graduation. I felt good about being able to do even that little bit for him. Mom made the funeral director put fleece-lined slippers on Pop's feet before he was buried. He hated it when his feet were cold.

Pop was seventy-five when he died, and he had been pallbearer for all his friends in the neighborhood. Now that there were no men his age still alive, his nephews and grandsons carried him to his grave. A cold, gusty wind was blowing, making it hard to keep the bunch of red roses we had put there from sliding off the coffin.

In November 1954, around Thanksgiving time, Mom fell in the kitchen and broke her hip. The break was set and pinned at the hospital in Iowa City, and she had just got home again when she had a stroke, and went into a coma from which she never recovered. On the day before Christmas, there was a terrible thunderstorm, unusual for that time of year in Iowa. A blinding flash of lightning was followed by a great crash of thunder. Mom opened her eyes, sat bolt upright and fell back dead. She was eighty-two years old.

Maude and Aubrey quit farming in the 1970s. For once their luck held, and they sold out before the drop in land prices that came in the early '80s. They got enough out of the farm to buy a little house in town, with money left over that kept them comfortable for the rest of their lives.

Aubrey died in August 1977. He had finished eating his Sunday noon meal, and around two o'clock he said he wasn't feeling very well. They drove him to the hospital at Iowa City, where he died about an hour later. He was seventy-nine. He had always said when he got to be eighty he hoped someone would shoot him.

Maude died four years later, in April 1981. She was eighty-four.

Today, of all the things I knew in the country as a boy, only the land itself is the same, although hills that were so steep and high then have been scraped down into gentle swells in a bland landscape.

Some of the farmsteads I knew have disappeared altogether. Hogan's and Kurth's farmhouses are gone; the old house on Hartz's second farm is no more; Dave Watson's pretty farmhouse, where Earl Gode and his wife lived before they retired, has been replaced with a mobile home, and my schoolmate Betty Lou Olsen's house and barn have vanished. The pioneer cemetery northwest of our farm, once a sandy hill covered with cockleburs and Spanish needles, is now green and well kept, but many of the white headstones have been vandalized or stolen. Aurora, the country school I attended, was torn down in 1953.

Ruth Schumacher Hahn lives down the hill north from the Timm farmstead, the last of my county schoolmates still in our neighborhood. She and her husband, Connie Hahn, own the nice old house where first the Ritchie family, and then Ernie Bell and his parents once lived.

Most of the fine old farmhouses are gone now. Some have been replaced with mobile homes, the best farmers can afford today in this, the richest part of the Midwest. Beautiful, well-maintained barns that were part of the landscape are neglected, unpainted and falling apart. Corncribs and granaries have been pulled down for the lumber that can be salvaged from them.

The farmers I knew when I was a boy were all suspicious of government. Is it possible they have been forced over to the enemy, resigning themselves to, "Get big or get out"? That is what seems to be happening: small farms gobbled up by larger farms are swallowed in turn by others larger still. The generally run-down look of houses and barns says one thing loud and clear, there isn't enough extra income on the finest land in the Midwest to pay for paint. Is this where all the political rant about the independence of farmers has led? What about those family values associated with small farms? What has happened to our sturdy pioneer principles now that the big fish so voraciously and conveniently eat the small ones?

Farms that used to support single families are now bunched into large units, a process that has been going on for years. In 1966 I spoke to our old friend and neighbor Everett Timm. Everett, who had farmed 200 acres, now said, "I'm farming 1,600 acres, and I'm not making it," and Everett was a first-class farmer, one who knew his business.

In spite of all I've written here about how much I disliked everything connected with farming, I had a secret boyhood dream of a magnificent layout, a dream I never revealed to anyone until now. My fantasy was that my family would own a full section, a square mile of land, 640 acres. It seemed to me that with so much land we would be rich beyond belief, but my old friend had just now told me he couldn't pay himself decent wages, and he was farming three times the acreage I had thought of as a kingdom.

During my visit Aubrey pointed out a John Deere rig: tractor, plow and disc standing in a neighbor's yard. He asked me, "How much do you think that cost?" I had no idea, and I shook my head. He answered his own question, "Over $80,000." That was in 1966. It gives you a hint as to the amount of capital a farm can gobble up today.

The old man, who had always goaded me because I didn't want to farm, now admitted, "If you've got enough money to start farming today, you're better off to invest it somewhere else." That was the way it had worked out for most of my Iowa friends. I know two men my age who are still on the farm.

Mixed farming is finished. The land in Iowa is given over to a one-crop economy. You see little livestock as you drive around the countryside: no horses, of course; God knows, no chickens; no sheep, synthetics have replaced wool in the textile industry; some cattle penned up in feeding yards and that's it. You don't see livestock grazing in pastures, because no land has been set aside for pasture. Every bit has been plowed up for what is now the only crop: corn. Not corn fed to hogs, cattle or sheep that might replenish farms with their manure, but corn sold off the land, the soil now fertilized with chemicals, petroleum-based additives that make possible yields of up to 400 bushels of corn to the acre, turning rivers and streams chocolate brown and edging stream banks with a thick layer of eroded topsoil.

Farm life in the 1930s and '40s had no frills about it. Threadbare is a word that might be used to describe the way we lived. Violence and brutality were part of our lives, too. We lived apart from each other, but farming then made us share the labor in major events like thrashing, making hay and filling silo. That kind of neighborly sharing helped balance the poverty and the alcohol-bred abuse that were also part of our lives. Good or bad, it is all gone today. Farmers no longer work together. There is no reason why they should.

The land still yields wealth, but it is hard to see where that wealth goes. It doesn't show on the remaining farmsteads, and it doesn't show in towns where the few farmers still working their land go to retire and die. The towns have been wrecked; there is no other way to put it. When I was a boy, the population of Marengo was 2,200. Today, with almost exactly the same number of people, Marengo is changed beyond recognition.

Look at what has happened to the town's businesses. During the 1930s, Marengo supported a half-dozen grocery stores: Drake's (later The Trading Post); Lindenmayer's; Fetzer's; Leib's; Gode's and Merrill's, each grocery store with its own meat market. We used to make fun of Mrs. Merrill's general store down at the depot where you could buy a little bit of almost anything, not realizing she had a tiny model for today's one-stop shopping centers.

Marengo had two good drug stores, each with its soda fountain: one run by a family named Eby, and the other by partners, Simmons and Sweezey. There were two farm implement dealerships: Bob Smith sold John Deere tractors and machinery, and Leo Kelly handled Allis-Chalmers farm equipment. We had five barbershops, reduced to four when old Mr. May died. And, of course, there were our two ice-cream parlors, the Greeks and Lindsay's.

As to health care, at one time Marengo had three doctors: Brown, Patterson, and Hollis; and three dentists: Black, Solbrig, and Galbraith. I went to Doc Black when I was about ten to get a cavity on the front of a tooth filled. It was considered innovative for him to fill it with porcelain instead of gold. Black told me the filling would probably last about ten years. Fifty years later, it was still holding firm, although it was perhaps a bit unsightly, when I had the tooth veneered. There is no dentist in Marengo today, and the town recently managed only with the greatest difficulty to find a doctor to work in its hospital.

Marengo once had six taverns and three pool halls. There were four filling stations in the center of town: Standard, Shell, Texaco and Mobil; gas pumps at three automobile dealerships: Ford, Chevrolet and Studebaker; plus four more filling stations scattered along the south edge of town.

Today, all the filling stations are gone from the center of town. Only Brown's Hardware, the bank and the weekly newspaper, The Pioneer-Republican (recently purchased by The Des Moines Register), Curley's Pool Hall, the Old Style Tavern (now up for sale—building and equipment—$60,000), and an all-but-dead Doose Hotel are still open, the few survivors from the 1930's.

Among those that have disappeared entirely are Gode's Dry Goods, Eby's Drugstore, Lawlors' clothing store, Simmons' Shoe Store, Bartusek's dry cleaners, a jewelry store, a furniture store, a liquor store, and a stationery shop called the "Square D" where school books were sold—all those places of business are gone today. Marengo formerly had several attorneys: Harold Swift, Hatter & Harnard, Byron Goldthwaite, Bert Stover, James Stapleton, and old Jim Dower. Today, I believe one attorney has an office in town.

All members of the Gode family—farmers, a trucker, a grocer and a dry-goods store proprietor—are dead. Earl Gode, the man who befriended me our first day on the farm, retired in the early '60's, and died a few years ago. The entire Gode Block, including the dry-goods store itself, sold for $25,000.

One drugstore is still in business, but there is no soda fountain, no candy store and no ice cream parlor. The picture show is long gone, killed by television. The Ford and Chevrolet dealerships, however, are still open and doing well.

At one time each of the businesses now vanished supported one or more families. When you talk about these things today, and ask what happened, people shrug and say, "Oh, now everybody drives to Cedar Rapids." It appears you have to blame the ruin of the town on comfortable cars and better roads, but greed may be the best explanation for the catastrophic changes in farming and in the wrecks of the small towns the farms supported.

Is it progress? I don't think so.

Odd Fellows' Cemetery
February 23, 1991

It was bitter at the cemetery, people were bundled up and shivering in their funeral best. Some little kid I didn't know was standing near the open grave. His mother asked him if he was cold. He said he was. Then he nodded toward the coffin and said, "I'll bet he's warm in there."

As a young man, Morey showed a great knack for restoring cars. It wasn't long before he had an auto-body shop of his own. He built up a reputation for knowing what he was doing, and people brought their classic-car restoration projects to him. Then, somewhere along the line, things started to go wrong. By the time he turned fifty, Morey had lost himself in a downward spiral, drinking heavily and sinking farther and farther into debt. One evening, late in the winter of 1990-'91, he told the woman he was living with that he was going out for cigarettes. He started his car in the closed garage and died there.

The minister, who had tried his best to give an appropriate talk at the funeral home and failed, came down the line of mourners, shaking hands with his gloves on. Morey had been an abusive father, but his two sons and his daughter—Bill, David (himself a suicide a few years later) and Brenda—stepped forward to lay their hands on the casket in a last gesture of farewell, and my brother's remains sank out of sight. None of us had got around to letting Morey know we loved him when he was alive.

One of his friends, a tough-looking fellow, leaned over and took a single pink blossom from the mound of flowers around the grave. He folded it into his handkerchief, tucked it in his jacket pocket and disappeared in the crowd.

The cars of Morey's funeral procession slipped away from the cemetery one by one. I walked over to the entrance gate, watching them disappear along US Highway 6. A few older people waved as they drove out, but I had been away for a good while, and most of the people there were strangers to me, even on sight.

Cars disappeared behind the hills east and west of the cemetery, the way we used to see train lights disappear when they left the depot, those lights and those people now long gone.

Morey's kids pulled their car up beside me at the gate. Bill rolled his window down.

"Do you need a lift, mister?"

"Yeah, I sure do."

The Author

Richard Willis grew up on a farm near Marengo, Iowa. As a professor of theater for 25 years, he taught and directed at Northwestern University, where he received his Ph.D., and at Lewis & Clark College, as chairman of the Department of Theater. He is published in *New Author's Journal*, *Words of Wisdom*, *Red Wheelbarrow*, *Phantasmagoria*, and *Iconoclast*. Richard taught soap opera technique to actors at the AFTRA workshop, and dramatic literature at the American Academy of Dramatic Art in New York. As a member of Actors' Equity, Screen Actors Guild, and the American Federation of Television and Radio Artists for the last twenty years he has appeared in movies, on TV, and in regional theater. His roles in feature films include *Drugstore Cowboy*, *Cops and Robbers*, and *The Last Innocent Man*. For three years he was seen on *One Life to Live*, as Asa Buchanan's butler, Nigel. Other recurring soap opera appearances include *All My Children* and *Another World*.

Richard lives in New York City with his wife, Linda, and two very nice cats.